They Meant Well

Government Project Disasters

D. R. MYDDELTON

T0162320

The Institute of Economic Affairs

First published in Great Britain in 2007 by
The Institute of Economic Affairs
2 Lord North Street
Westminster
London SW1P 3LB
in association with Profile Books Ltd

The mission of the Institute of Economic Affairs is to improve public understanding of the fundamental institutions of a free society, by analysing and expounding the role of markets in solving economic and social problems.

A CIP catalogue record for this book is available from the British Library.

ISBN 978 0 255 36601 4

Many IEA publications are translated into languages other than English or are reprinted. Permission to translate or to reprint should be sought from the Director General at the address above.

Typeset in Stone by MacGuru Ltd
info@macguru.org.uk

Printed and bound in Great Britain by Hobbs the Printers

CONTENTS

THE AUTHOR

D. R. Myddelton was educated at Eton and the Harvard Business School. He is a chartered accountant. Since 1972 he has been Professor of Finance and Accounting at the Cranfield School of Management (Emeritus since retiring in 2005). He has for many years been a member of the Council of the University of Buckingham and since 2001 has been chairman of the managing trustees of the Institute of Economic Affairs.

Professor Myddelton has written many books and articles and has contributed to IEA publications on accounting, inflation and taxation. His textbooks include *The Meaning of Company Accounts* (8th edition, 2005), with Professor Walter Reid, and *Managing Business Finance* (2000). He has also written *On a Cloth Untrue: Inflation Accounting, the Way Forward* (1984); *The Power to Destroy: A Study of the British Tax System* (2nd edition, 1994); and *Unshackling Accountants* (2004).

FOREWORD

When it comes to the involvement of government in large-scale investment projects, we continually seem to relive history. This monograph, *They Meant Well: government project disasters*, looks in detail at six large-scale government, quasi-commercial projects over the last 85 years and finds that serious mismanagement, combined with obfuscation and an unwillingness to be accountable to those whose money was being spent, led to an enormous waste of taxpayers' money.

Some of these projects, such as the groundnut scheme, were recognised to be disasters at a relatively early stage and were wound up in a decade or less, but others rumbled on, losing money over more than a generation without anybody having the courage to bring the project to an end. Indeed, the nuclear power programme has been going on for 50 years and it looks as if it will continue, with state support, for another generation.

The author, D. R. Myddelton, chose deliberately narrow criteria for determining which projects to include in this monograph, but the problems he identifies in these case studies have much wider ramifications for the operation of government. For example, the various governments that submitted bids to host the 2012 Olympic Games seemed to be competing on the basis of the amount of public money that they could manage to spend: prestige of government ministers and officials came before accountability to the taxpayer and the assessment of risks and profit and loss. Recent government IT projects, hybrid rail schemes such as the West Coast Mainline upgrade and the Scottish Parliament building all exhibit aspects of the problems identified by the author in the case studies.

It seems that government officials and politicians have a very narrow view of how to determine the net benefits of the projects they propose. They stress the value of everything and the cost of nothing. In the projects discussed in this monograph, arguments such as job creation, the social benefits of research and development, and the reduced cost of imports are all advanced in favour of a particular government-backed, quasi-commercial project. But the politicians and bureaucrats forget that there are jobs squeezed out because of the costs of financing a project, that resources expended on research and development in one field can mean that fewer resources are available in another industry, or that reducing the imports of one product can raise the real exchange rate and make it harder for exporters to export their products.

As has been noted, the story of the failure of these projects is one of mismanagement, blurred lines of responsibility and lack of accountability. But, as the author makes clear, there are good economic reasons why projects are likely to be mismanaged in the public sector. Resources are better used in the private sector, where economic actors have dispersed information that cannot be centralised by government. The incentives for success and to achieve a particular objective at the lowest possible cost are also much greater in the private sector than in the public sector. Also, once a project is started, it is very difficult for politicians and bureaucrats to decide to give up on the project and wind it up.

Much better that this process is delayed so that the embarrassment happens on somebody else's watch.

Public choice economics is also important. Perhaps the most blatant example of how economic resources can be misallocated as a result of political pressure was in a project that is mentioned briefly by the author: the building of the Humber Bridge. The Humber Bridge was promised quite specifically to the people of Hull to win a by-election. When the bridge opened in 1981, I remember the Lord Mayor of Hull saying words to the effect of: 'people complain that the bridge is too much of a luxury in these difficult economic times, but who complains about a luxury from time to time?' Perhaps the people whose jobs were crowded out of the private sector in order to provide the resources to build the bridge might have complained; and the then-future generations of taxpayers who have to pay for it are still complaining – as evidenced by the websites that still exist to persuade the government to relieve the debt by moving it from local taxpayers (who demanded the bridge) to taxpayers in general (who did not).

The history of public sector, quasi-commercial projects is financial disaster caused by mismanagement, encouraged by an economic framework that does not provide the right incentives for the dissemination of information about costs and benefits. Sadly, public choice economics also suggests that we may relive that history again and again. But this monograph, which is both readable and enjoyable, will help arm future generations with the arguments against the government spending other people's money to achieve commercial objectives. Thus, armed with its arguments and evidence, perhaps we can ensure that future generations of politicians and bureaucrats are more prudent than their forebears.

The views expressed in this monograph are, as in all IEA publications, those of the author and not those of the Institute (which has no corporate view), its managing trustees, Academic Advisory Council members or senior staff.

PHILIP BOOTH

Editorial and Programme Director,
Institute of Economic Affairs
Professor of Insurance and Risk Management,
Sir John Cass Business School, City University
July 2007

ACKNOWLEDGEMENTS

Perhaps because of its variety, I have derived more pleasure from writing this book than from any other I can remember. One advantage of retirement is that you can take your time about writing. So my thanks to Philip Booth for encouraging me to do the book, and for waiting somewhat longer than planned for me to complete it (though not, however, long enough to meet one of my criteria for a project's 'failure'!). I am grateful to the following for help and advice: Ruth Bender, John Blundell, Robert Boyd, Peter Clarke, Chris Edwards, Robert Miller, John Raybould, Murray Steele, Chris van der Hoven and Christian Wignall. I would particularly like to thank my brother Roger for commenting on a draft version of the book. Two academic referees made constructive comments which were appreciated. I am also grateful to Cranfield library staff and to Thea Hughes, my former secretary at Cranfield, for help in tracking down several of the sources.

SUMMARY

- Government officials and ministers usually mean well when they promote and manage quasi-commercial projects in the public sector, which however often turn out to be financial disasters. Any technological advances come at huge expense.
- A recurring rationale for grandiose projects, from the groundnut scheme to the Millennium Dome, has been to boost 'national prestige', but this concept has little real value.
- The costs of ventures dependent on new, untried technology, such as the R.101 airship or nuclear power, are extremely uncertain, so taxpayers have to underwrite their high risks. Initial financial estimates may often be purposely too low.
- Partly due to changes in specifications, many of the projects incurred time and cost overruns of more than 100 per cent. The high speed Channel Tunnel Rail Link is still not ready more than thirteen years after the Tunnel itself opened.
- The absence of market pressures in the UK's civil nuclear power programme meant that nobody knew or cared how much it was costing. The result was total losses far exceeding those of all the other five projects together.
- State projects are always liable to short-term political interference, which may increase costs, as for the Millennium Dome, or risks, as for the R.101 airship.
- The government's opaque accounting practices often disguise

the true level of state spending on large projects, as with the Channel Tunnel Rail Link.

- Governments do not understand markets, and on some projects, such as Concorde, made little effort to research likely customer demand.
- In the market system investors bear the costs of ventures that fail, but in the political system taxpayers have to do so. As a result, governments often choose to continue projects such as the groundnut scheme and Concorde, even after it has become clear they are not commercially viable.
- None of the six projects was well managed and many of the failures were down to politicians: installing inadequate or over-complex organisations, appointing incompetent managers, or insisting on excessive secrecy.

TABLES

PREFACE

Here are brief accounts of six large British government quasi-commercial twentieth-century projects which all 'went wrong' in one way or another: the R.101 airship; the groundnut scheme; nuclear power; Concorde; the Channel Tunnel; and the Millennium Dome.

Adam Smith famously described how every individual is often led by an invisible hand to promote an end – namely the public interest – which was no part of his intention. In this book I discuss the other side of that coin: people who end up making things worse, not better, despite their good intentions. Each of the six projects aimed to promote the national interest, but each resulted in huge losses. Smith himself said: 'I have never known much good done by those who affected to trade for the public good.'[1]

The title *They Meant Well* stems from a conversation long ago with Ralph Harris. He said something about 'do-gooders', and I had the temerity to correct him: 'They're not "do-gooders", but "mean-wellers".' Almost certainly nearly everyone involved in these projects that 'went wrong' *did* mean well. One cannot read about these projects (still less write about them) without being conscious of the huge efforts many dedicated people made over a period of years. But '… *good men who work very hard at their jobs,*

---

1   Adam Smith, *The Wealth of Nations*, 1776, Book IV, ch. II.

in certain institutional conditions, *can and do make an awful botch of things.*[2] The fact is, the cost of the input does not determine the value of the output. 'It is not that pearls fetch a high price because men have dived for them; but on the contrary, men dive for them because they fetch a high price.'[3]

Each of these large government projects lasted for several years and cost the taxpayer far more money than originally expected. There are some common factors, but each project has its unique aspects. Part of the fascination of these complex 'case studies' is that they combine politics and economics, technology and management. I thought it might be of interest to students of management, politics and markets to read brief but fairly comprehensive accounts; and I have also tried to draw some general conclusions.

I had long been familiar with Nevil Shute's account of the R.101 disaster in his autobiography *Slide Rule* and with Alan Wood's book about the early years of 'The Ground Nut Affair'. Both were dramatic stories which rather downplayed the financial aspects. I was also aware of a number of books on Concorde and on the Channel Tunnel, several of which seemed to emphasise technical or environmental angles. At least two books about the Millennium Dome appeared before the Dome itself even opened, covering only the earlier part of that project's life.

Like most laymen, I knew very little about the nuclear power programmes. Not only was I ignorant about the technology, but I also had no idea how much money they had 'lost'. (I was not then aware that the Atomic Energy Authority had also been very hazy about costs.) So I am most grateful to Professor Colin Robinson,

---

2   William A. Niskanen, *Bureaucracy: Servant or Master?*, IEA, London, 1973, p. 4.

3   Richard Whately, *Introductory Essays on Political Economy*, Dublin, 1832, p. 253.

who made a substantial contribution to Chapter 4 on nuclear power, based on his own book.[4]

Most of the key facts about these projects are in the public domain. I have used published sources (see Appendix 1), doing virtually no personal interviews and little original research. Where possible I have tried to check facts from more than one source, though sometimes one source merely repeats another. Responsibility for any errors is mine. Because I have gone into a fair amount of detail, at least a few of my 'facts' may turn out to be wrong; but I hope and expect that will not much affect the overall picture.

As a rule there is only a short description of operations, once the 'project' itself is complete. The Millennium Dome is an exception, mainly because of its severe financial problems during the year 2000. In my view the Channel Tunnel 'project' finishes in 2007, with the opening of the high-speed link to London, rather than in 1994 with the completion of the Tunnel itself.

I have included money amounts where possible, but they are only approximate. Sources can vary, and the accuracy of the accounting is not always beyond doubt. In order to compare the various projects' costs in 'real' terms, throughout the book I have used the Retail Prices Index, or its pre-1947 equivalent, to adjust key amounts into terms of 2007 pounds.

There are many different acronyms, especially for nuclear power and the Channel Tunnel. I have tried not to overuse them, but they *are* convenient. Because of their extent, it seems helpful to list them at the end of each chapter as well as all together at the end.

---

4   *The Power of the State*, Adam Smith Institute, 1991 (especially chs 1 and 3).

Chapter 1, the Introduction, very briefly describes each project, explains how the book compares money amounts for them, and interprets each aspect of 'large British government quasi-commercial projects which "went wrong" in the last hundred years'. There follows a discussion of the meaning of 'opportunity cost' in the context of both corporate and government projects, a discussion of economic problems inherent in government projects and a brief outline of general arguments for and against nationalisation (state ownership) of industries.

Chapters 2 to 7 then comprise detailed accounts of each of the six projects in chronological order. They aim to cover political, technical, organisational, commercial and financial aspects of each project. These chapters can be read in any order, but the concluding chapters, 8, 9 and 10, will be more meaningful if the reader is familiar with the details of Chapters 2 to 7.

Chapter 8 discusses aspects of government, Chapter 9 costs and benefits, and Chapter 10 attempts to draw some general conclusions.

Finally there is a note on the main sources I have used and a full list of acronyms.

They Meant Well

Government Project Disasters

1 INTRODUCTION

Six projects that went wrong

Here are brief accounts of six large British government quasi-commercial projects in the last hundred years. The projects differ widely in size and nature, but they all 'went wrong' for various reasons. They were important enough for the government of the day to regard each of them as involving 'national prestige'.

The six projects are:

- The R.101 airship (1922 to 1930)
- The groundnut scheme (1946 to 1954)
- Nuclear power (1955 to 1978 to …)
- Concorde (1956 to 1976 to 2003)
- The Channel Tunnel (1964 to 1975, and 1985 to 1994 to 2007)
- The Millennium Dome (1994 to 2000)

The R.101 was a post-World War I imperial project to connect by airship the main cities of the British Empire. The groundnut scheme was a post-World War II colonial project to reduce Britain's food bill and help develop a large backward area of Africa. Nuclear power, Concorde and the Channel Tunnel were three huge projects, each covering most of the second half of the twentieth century. Concorde was the odd one out of the three, in that it was never aimed at a mass market. The Millennium Dome evoked memories of the 1851 Great Exhibition in Hyde Park and the 1951 Festival of Britain on the South Bank.

There are some points of resemblance between projects:

- The R.101 airship, nuclear power and Concorde were all projects on the frontiers of knowledge – which are also the frontiers of ignorance. The costs of such projects can be extremely difficult to estimate in advance.
- All three of the very large projects – nuclear power, Concorde and the Channel Tunnel – were subject to public environmental objections.
- Concorde and the Channel Tunnel involved Anglo-French partnerships – a phrase which alerts *tout le monde* to possible trouble. Both were 'cancelled' by the British at one point, but were completed in the end.

Commercial projects normally aim to achieve profit (= 'success') and to avoid loss (= 'failure'). By profit we mean 'economic profit', not merely 'accounting profit' – in other words, after charging a notional 'cost of equity capital': interest on debt capital, or borrowed money, will already have been charged as an expense in the accounts. Government projects, however, even 'quasi-commercial' ones, may not aim to make a profit. For example, regardless of profit or loss the French clearly wanted Concorde to help build up their own aircraft industry. Nor did the British government really care whether the Dome made a 'profit' or not, though it may have lost more than expected.

The next six chapters (2 to 7) deal with each of the projects in chronological order. The past may be a foreign country where they do things differently, but many of the pressures seem familiar. No doubt critical comment is easier with hindsight. But '... a great deal that can be seen today could also be seen yesterday. Fear of exploiting the benefit of hindsight is a great, but often unjustified, protector of reputations'.[1]

Not everyone would regard each of these projects as a failure. Roy Jenkins, for instance, was Minister of Aviation in October 1964. He had to tell the French government that the new British Labour government was cancelling the Concorde project (on cost grounds) – before uncancelling it three months later. Writing in 1991, he regarded it as 'open to argument' whether dropping the project would really have been a good idea.[2]

Three of the projects are now history. The genesis of the R.101 airship – aiming to link major cities of the British Empire – occurred in 1922, when David Lloyd George was prime minister. The post-war groundnut scheme in Tanganyika emerged in 1946, the first year of Clement Attlee's premiership. Its name still denotes a classic fiasco. Even the Concorde project, which finished recently in a sentimental haze, started more than half a century ago in 1956, at the time of Suez and Anthony Eden.

The other three projects are more recent and still in the news, even in 2007. Many of the second nuclear power programme's stations are currently in use, though British Energy (65 per cent government-owned) has had recent trouble with several of the reactors. The second phase of the Channel Tunnel's high-speed rail link to London is finally due to open this year (2007); while Eurotunnel has recently refinanced its outstanding loans yet again, partly at the expense of its (mostly French) small equity

1   Edmund Dell, *The Chancellors*, HarperCollins, London, 1996, p. 10.
2   Roy Jenkins, *A Life at the Centre*, Macmillan, Basingstoke, 1991, p. 166.

shareholders. Meanwhile talks are still under way about the Millennium Dome's possible use as a giant casino.

It will be helpful to compare some financial aspects of these six projects, so I begin with an important technical point relating to money.

Comparing money amounts

The first sentence of Jane Austen's *Pride and Prejudice* is famous: 'It is a truth universally acknowledged that a single man in possession of a good fortune, must be in want of a wife.' A 'good fortune' later turned out to be 'four or five thousand [pounds] a year'. Today that amount of money is about the same as a single person's annual state pension, which nobody would call a 'fortune'. Admittedly the book first appeared in 1813, two years before Waterloo; and no doubt many readers would expect it to be tricky trying to compare money amounts nearly two hundred years apart.

As it happens, however, the purchasing power of the pound sterling was much the same on the outbreak of World War I in 1914 as it had been at the Restoration of Charles II in 1660. Apart from the period around the Napoleonic Wars, that meant *a quarter of a millennium* of stable money, which established the Bank of England's former reputation for monetary soundness. (Samuel Pepys could have discussed the cost of living with the young Maynard Keynes!) But the pound's performance over the last hundred years has been very different[3] and there has been massive

---

3   Dating almost precisely from Keynes's foolish comment in his first book, *Indian Currency and Finance*, Macmillan, Basingstoke, 1913, p. 51: 'A preference for a gold currency is no longer more than a relic of a time when governments were less trustworthy in these matters than they are now …'

inflation. So in our lifetimes it has indeed become extremely difficult to compare money amounts over time.

In particular, unprecedented currency debasement in the fifteen years from 1965 to 1980 greatly affected the money costs of three very large projects during this period: nuclear power, Concorde and the (first) Channel Tunnel. The pound's purchasing power halved between 1945 and 1965; it halved again between 1965 and 1975; and it halved *again* between 1975 and 1980. Thus the historical 'half-life' of the pound was twenty years in 1965, ten years in 1975 and a mere five years in 1980. Today – 2007 – it is again just under twenty years. (The Retail Prices Index [January 1987 = 100] reached 200 in September 2006.) That means money would lose nearly 90 per cent of its purchasing power in a lifetime of eighty years: still hardly respectable, but less devastating than in the 1970s.

For each project, current money amounts of the time are reported in normal font. But on occasion the book shows money amounts adjusted by means of the Retail Prices Index[4] into terms of the purchasing power of today's (2007) pounds. These 'real' amounts are shown in **bold**. Such adjustments are essential to give readers today an idea of the relative financial size of the six projects.

I need hardly say that these 'constant purchasing power' amounts can only be very approximate. The margin of error could easily be plus or minus 10 per cent – *or more*. I have used the following range of factors – based on the Retail Prices Index – to translate current pounds for each project into 2007 pounds:

---

4   For a discussion of which index to use, see D. R. Myddelton: *On a Cloth Untrue: Inflation accounting, the way forward*, Woodhead-Faulkner, 1984, pp. 55–9.

The scope of the book

The book's scope is limited to large British government quasi-commercial projects that 'went wrong' in the last hundred years.

'Large'

Three of the projects were very large, in terms of both money and time. Nuclear power, Concorde and the (second) Channel Tunnel each cost at least **£10,000 million** and construction lasted more than ten years (including the Channel Tunnel high-speed rail link to London). The groundnut scheme and the Millennium Dome were 'medium-size' projects, costing about **£1,000 million** and lasting several years in total. The least costly was the R.101 airship, for which the whole programme (including the R.100) cost 'only' about **£100 million**; but even that project lasted more than six years. All the projects involved at least two different ministries, in addition to the Treasury (always) and the Foreign Office (often).

'British'

This book looks at British projects that went wrong (though two of them also involved the French government as partners). But other countries too have experienced disastrous large projects: for example, the Sydney Opera House in Australia (ten years late and **£500 million** over budget), the Honshu–Hokkaido tunnel in Japan (ten years late and **£2,000 million** over budget) and the San Francisco Bay Area Rapid Transit system in the United States (**£2,750 million** over budget).

'Government'

Making a profit is the *raison d'être* of commercial enterprise, and company directors must account to shareholders for their success or failure in doing so. Government quasi-commercial projects may aim to make a profit, but if they fail, taxpayers have to pick up the tab. Inability or unwillingness to abandon projects even when it has become clear they are going to make huge losses – in effect throwing good money after bad – is perhaps more likely to be a fault of governments, for whom saving political 'face' may seem all-important.

'Quasi-commercial'

By 'quasi-commercial' I mean projects that aim to benefit the public directly either by reducing costs or by providing services for which sales revenues exceed total costs. Other British government post-war projects may have been very costly, even 'disastrous', but many have been omitted because they were not quasi-commercial; for instance:

- the British National Library (three times over budget and many years late);
- the Humber Bridge (175 per cent cost overrun) – whereby a politician, Barbara Castle, used taxpayers' money to help win a by-election in Hull North in January 1966;
- the Scottish Parliament building (costing **£500 million**, a tenfold increase over the original estimate, and completed three years late);
- the Thames Barrier (costing **£1,100 million** and completed three and a half years late).

In all the above cases there was a definite end-product. In contrast, government computer projects, such as for the London Ambulance Service or the Passport Office (and other government IT disasters still in progress, such as for the National Health Service), are indirect means of providing government services that are not themselves sold to the public. Military projects that have gone wrong have been excluded for the same reason, e.g. Blue Streak, TSR-2, Nimrod and many others.

'Projects'

The 'nationalised' (state) industries were large government quasi-commercial undertakings, but these ongoing concerns do not qualify as 'projects'. Nor can a government enterprise such as the Industrial Reorganisation Corporation (from 1966 to 1971) be regarded as a single project; and it would hardly be fair to pick out its 'failures' while ignoring the successes in its portfolio. The three largest projects all involved (then) nationalised industries: nuclear power and both the Central Electricity Generating Board and the South of Scotland Electricity Board; Concorde and the British Overseas Airways Corporation (later British Airways); and the Channel Tunnel with the high-speed rail link and British Rail (and its successors).

'Which went wrong'

What does 'going wrong' imply? One or more of the following, compared with plan:

- Failure to deliver the end-product (R.101 airship; groundnut scheme)
- Customer demand much less than expected (Concorde; Channel Tunnel; Millennium Dome)
- Taking much longer to complete than planned (R.101 airship; nuclear power; Concorde; Channel Tunnel[5])
- Net cost to government much higher than budget (all six projects)

It is true that these criteria are not completely independent. If a project takes far longer than expected, it may not be surprising that the net cost to government is much higher than budget; similarly if a project fails to produce an end-product.

'In the past hundred years'

I am not aware of similar government projects from more than a hundred years ago. Before 1900 taxes normally took under 10 per

---

5   Including the Channel Tunnel high-speed link to London.

cent of the national income and much of that comprised interest on past borrowings to finance wars. (The proportion in 1900 itself, at 10 per cent, was unusually high, owing to the Boer War.) British governments, in those days, tended to minimise their role, not (as now) to maximise it. They usually preferred not to get involved in quasi-commercial projects at all. For instance, it was profit-seeking private companies which built the railways in early Victorian times, not the government. And the Great Exhibition of 1851 does not qualify for two reasons. First, it was a financial success (profit about **£12 million**); and second, with the organising committee chaired by Prince Albert, it was financed by private enterprise. The government refused to shoulder the cost of 'frivolities'.[6]

Opportunity cost

Money invested in one project is no longer available to invest in other, possibly better, projects. So it is always important to be aware of hypothetical other ways in which the money could have been spent. The forgone benefit from the 'next best' project that the money could have been spent on represents a project's 'opportunity cost'. This applies to governments as well as to profit-seeking companies.

The Discounted Cash Flow (DCF) method of evaluation sets out the amount and timing of the project's expected incremental future cash receipts and payments. These are then 'discounted' (to 'present value' terms) by applying a suitable discount rate representing the estimated 'opportunity cost' of capital. If total discounted cash inflows exceed total discounted cash outflows,

6   Daphne Bennett, *King without a Crown*, Century, London, 1977, p. 200.

then the project promises a positive 'net present value' (NPV), and should be worth investing in. That is the theory. In practice, both the amount and the timing of the expected future cash flows – as well as the discount rate itself – are usually subject to a large margin of error. So by no means all projects that 'promise' a positive NPV end up making a profit.

It can be hard to tell what discount rate to use. It may be helpful to split the discount rate into three parts: pure time preference, inflation premium and risk premium. Pure time preference is normally assumed to be about 2 per cent a year; though recent yields on index-linked gilts have been much lower. Many people prefer to express cash flows in 'real' terms (of 'constant Year 0 purchasing power'), *excluding* inflation (rather than in 'money' terms, including inflation); in which case there is no need to include an inflation premium in the discount rate.

Governments may be able to borrow at low interest rates, because people think lending to them is 'risk free'. Governments that control the printing presses[7] are almost certain to repay money they have borrowed since they can simply print it! What that amount of money will be worth in real terms, if there is inflation, is quite another matter – as many people who lent to governments in the past know only too well.

But the risk of the *project*, not the *investor*'s overall risk profile, should determine what risk premium to include in the discount rate. For example, commercial companies should use a *low* risk premium to assess low-risk projects – even though their own corporate weighted average cost of capital may include a fairly high risk premium to cover the 'average' risk of all their business.

---

7   These no longer include EU member states in the Euro Area, whose borrowing may thus be 'risky' even in money terms.

Hence if *governments* are thinking of investing in 'risky' projects then they do need to add a suitable 'risk premium' to pure time preference. (That surely applied to each of the six projects in this book.) This should give the 'real risky discount rate' to apply to the expected future cash flows. Where a project is so risky that private companies are not willing to invest in it, clearly it should carry a large risk premium. This will result in a high overall discount rate, which means the project is unlikely to promise a positive NPV. It may then be hard for a government to 'justify' investing in such a project on commercial grounds.

In practice it is extremely difficult either for companies or for governments to quantify the appropriate risk premium for complex projects. But at least companies can estimate how a large project's success or failure might affect profits, dividends payable and financial gearing. These are all things in which financial markets take a keen interest. In contrast, tax or borrowing levels matter much less to governments; and anyway the economic impact of even a large project on either would be small. Thus governments have much less *incentive* than companies to act commercially. Neither profits nor losses matter nearly as much to governments as they do to commercial companies.

Economic problems inherent in government projects

In the market consumers choose how to spend their money and producers anticipate or respond to consumer demand. The prospect of profit gives companies an incentive to develop new products or new methods of production; while the risk of loss also provides an incentive to drop product lines that no longer promise good returns. When company managers take bad decisions, shareholders can respond by selling their shares, which may trigger a change in management. Companies that manage investment projects well are more likely to prosper; whereas those that do not will need to change direction or else they may suffer takeover or, in the extreme, bankruptcy.

Admittedly it is not always easy to get company managements (agents) to act in the interests of shareholders (owners/principals). For example:

- Managers like companies to grow in size (which often partly determines their pay); but shareholders want economic profit (after allowing for the cost of equity capital).
- Managers like retaining equity capital in the business, instead of paying it out in dividends, to give themselves leeway; shareholders, in contrast, like getting dividends and, if need be, prefer using higher levels of debt to discipline managers.
- Managers often like exciting new ventures; whereas shareholders would rather companies stick to what they know.
- Managers like diversification (partly for size reasons, partly to reduce their personal risk); but shareholders can diversify their own portfolios if they want to.

Companies often succeed in making large profits from commercial projects, but profit-seeking companies have sometimes experienced disasters too: in America, the Ford Edsel lost at least $200 million (**£1,200 million**), and General Dynamics lost $425 million (**£1,800 million**) on its Convair 880 and 990 jet airliners. More recently Long Term Capital Management lost $4.5 billion (**£3,300 million**) in less than a year. In the UK, Wembley

Stadium has been a recent expensive disaster – though whether the disaster would have been as expensive if it were not for the interference of local and national government is a moot point. And many (perhaps most) large private sector mergers go wrong, from the viewpoint of shareholders in the acquiring company, partly for the reasons listed above.

Despite such principal/agent problems, the private sector normally ensures that in the long run managers have regard to the interests of shareholders. But in the public sector there are no such means to enable taxpayers to hold politicians to account. Failure of one quasi-commercial government project, however large, seems unlikely to lose decisive votes at a future general election. Governing parties have to account only every four or five years on a whole miscellany of past actions. Their appeal to voters largely comprises actual or implied promises for the future, and perhaps some unchanging principles too. So it is hard to provide effective incentives to get governments to act in the interests of the people as a whole.[8] All one can really hope for under modern democratic systems is a chance from time to time to 'throw the rascals out', for whatever reasons. And even that sometimes hardly applies – for instance, with respect to the European Commission.

Moreover certain interest groups, expecting to gain substantial benefits from a government project, may be willing to invest time and money in pressing for it to continue. But taxpayers who collectively bear the costs of government projects lose such a small amount each that nobody thinks it worthwhile to campaign against them. (A similar argument applies to 'single issue' groups.)

---

[8]   See Gordon Tullock, *The Vote Motive*, rev. edn, IEA, London, 2006.

Another reason why government projects are less likely to succeed than those in the private sector stems from the age-old argument about 'economic calculation'. Without markets the government cannot determine a specific project's value to potential consumers. In contrast, the private sector, responding to price signals, constantly looks for a way to add value for consumers – and ultimately shareholders. As part of the process of competition, different companies seek least-cost ways to fulfil consumers' preferences. This does not mean the private sector will never fail, of course, since trial and error is central to the market system.

The government might feel the need for involvement if there were a natural monopoly, though that hardly applies to any of our six projects. Some people might argue for government action on the grounds that the relevant scientific research is a public good;[9] but the government could subsidise such research without tying it to a particular project. In fact the number of genuine public goods that the private sector cannot provide is very small.[10]

Nationalisation

There was widespread nationalisation (state ownership of industries) in the UK after World War II, which lasted until the 1980s. Some of our projects were undertaken during that time of nationalisation. Many of the arguments for and against nationalisation were also used in the debates about whether the government should undertake the various projects that we examine below.

---

9   But see Terence Kealey, *The Economic Laws of Scientific Research*, Macmillan, Basingstoke, 1996.

10   See Arthur Seldon, 'Introducing market forces into "public" services', *Collected Works*, vol. 4, Liberty Fund, Indianapolis, IN, 2005.

The nationalised industries also had similar financial outcomes to those of the projects discussed in this book.

The original reasons[11] for nationalisation no longer seem very convincing, but may be relevant to the question of government versus private enterprise:

- *Government control of the 'commanding heights' of the economy helps effective national planning.* This reason is now out of fashion, possibly because the 'commanding heights' all too often turned into bottomless pits.
- *Nationalisation replaces wasteful private profit-seeking rivalry with public-spirited enterprise.* Any business that cannot go bankrupt has little incentive not to waste money. Moreover competition gives customers standards by which to judge quality.
- *Only the government can provide the huge amounts of finance for capital-intensive industries.* In the end, however, government can get capital only from lenders, taxpayers or consumers.
- *Many of the state industries are technical monopolies, which, in private hands, might abuse their position.* But the railways and the coal mines were kept going by governments only too anxious to protect them from competition. Privatisation has shown that competition can flourish even in the utilities.
- *Many of the loss-making services of state industries are worth having for 'social' reasons.* If need be, taxpayers (via government) can subsidise consumers directly.

---

11 This list comes from D. R. Myddelton, *Denationalization – the Problem of Recapitalising*, Aims of Industry, 1970, pp. 2/3. It was gleaned from various socialist politicians such as Herbert Morrison and Hugh Gaitskell, as discussed (for example) in R. Kelf-Cohen, *Twenty Years of Nationalisation*, Macmillan, Basingstoke, 1969, chs 1 and 13.

These state monopolies could charge higher prices to compensate for inefficiencies. And often poor performance would result in lower quality for the captive customers. For example, the Post Office (then also including telephones) made a real profit – but the memory still lingers of having to wait for many months before being granted the privilege of getting a (black) telephone. On the other hand there were strong political reasons for keeping down commuter fares, so British Rail's losses did not always reflect poor performance alone.

Early in my career I wrote an article[12] showing the real losses after interest of all the main nationalised industries after allowing for inflation. The losses – using 254 sets of annual accounts over the 22-year period 1948–70 – were as follows (in today's [2007] purchasing power): coal **£6,500 million**; electricity **£2,200 million**; gas **£2,500 million**; rail **£28,000 million**; others **£3,300 million**. The Post Office (including telephones) made a *profit* of **£2,500 million**. The total real losses after interest for all the nationalised industries together were **£40,000 million**, in 2007 pounds. This represents an average of more than **£1,800 million** a year for 22 years.

Not only were the financial results extremely poor, and in contravention of the 1961 instruction to 'break even taking one year with another'; but the *quality* of services also left much to be desired. We should not forget the damage to the economy from inadequate transport, inefficient communications, needlessly expensive electricity, etc.

The official attitude to technology seems to vary between

12   D. R. Myddelton, 'Consolidated nationalised industries accounts 1948–70: published figures adjusted for currency debasement', *Accounting and Business Review*, Spring 1972, pp. 83–109.

complacency and trendiness. The former is illustrated by the Admiralty's alleged response[13] to the invention of the electric telegraph, to the effect that they were perfectly content with their semaphore system! The latter is illustrated by Lord Beeching's comment[14] that the British government 'has wasted an enormous amount of money on things justified by the pursuit of advanced technology – an almost childlike desire to play with toys'.

---

13 Herbert Spencer, *The Man versus the State*, Penguin, Harmondsworth, 1969, p. 127.

14 Quoted in John Jewkes, *Government and High Technology*, IEA, London, 1972, p. 11.

2 THE R.101 AIRSHIP (1922–30)

Background

As late as 1922 most people thought aeroplanes would never be suitable for flying passengers long distances, since heavier-than-air machines were low-powered, very noisy and unpleasant to travel in. Instead it seemed more likely that lighter-than-air airships, while possibly unsuitable for military purposes, would operate all the civil transoceanic routes. In contrast to aeroplanes, they could be both quiet and comfortable – 'floating rather than flying'. At that time the largest aeroplanes carried only a dozen passengers with a range of 250 miles. No aeroplane had yet crossed the Atlantic from east to west; but a German airship, the *Graf Zeppelin*, was already carrying commercial loads of passengers to South America.

A leading advocate of airships was Dennis Burney, Conservative MP for Uxbridge. In 1922 he proposed that Vickers should build six commercial airships and operate them on empire routes, with a taxpayer subsidy of £400,000 a year for seven years. The first airship would make a demonstration flight to India, where no airship had ever flown before. Then Vickers would build five more to provide a regular mail and passenger service to Egypt and India. This could later extend beyond Karachi to Rangoon, Singapore and Perth. There could also be a regular service between England and North America.

The new Vickers airships would be twice the size of any previous lighter-than-air craft: their volume would be 5 million cubic feet (760 feet long and 110 feet wide). Burney optimistically reckoned they would be able to fly for 3,000 miles at 80 mph, carrying 200 passengers in luxury, and 10 tons of mail. They would take only about three days to reach India, a full fortnight less than the seventeen-day sea voyage. An important part of the project would be to construct a number of large mooring masts: initially these would be at Cardington, near Bedford, Montreal in Canada, Ismailia in Egypt and Karachi in India.[1]

In July 1922, David Lloyd George's coalition government set up a committee (chaired by Leo Amery from the Admiralty) to consider the financial aspects of Burney's airship proposal. There was also an advisory panel to examine technical and operational matters, including both Burney himself and Brigadier-General C. B. Thomson. A year later the committee (now with Sir Samuel Hoare, air minister, as chairman) recommended going ahead, with an annual subsidy of £250,000, and the cabinet accepted its report.

Masefield[2] says this decision in favour of private enterprise was against the advice of Air Ministry officials and against the *advisory panel*'s majority view; but Viscount Templewood[3] (formerly Sir Samuel Hoare) says the *committee*'s view was unanimous in favour. In any event, Baldwin's Conservative government lost office in December 1923 before it could sign an agreement. So the first-ever Labour government came in for a short period, under Ramsay MacDonald, as the third government in little over a year.

---

1   Karachi was then in India, as Pakistan became a separate country only in 1947.
2   Sir Peter Masefield, *To Ride the Storm: The Story of the Airship R.101*, William Kimber, London, 1982, p. 452.
3   Viscount Templewood, *Empire of the Air: The Advent of the Air Age, 1922–1929*, Collins, London, 1957, p. 221.

The new Secretary of State for Air was C. B. Thomson, now Lord Thomson of Cardington, the first trained engineer to reach cabinet rank. (He had twice been an unsuccessful Labour candidate at general elections.) He was not at all keen on the Vickers proposal, which he thought might end in a private monopoly. So in March 1924 he proposed[4] an airships programme for 'Government Research, Experiment and Development'. Under its aegis the Air Ministry would design and construct an advanced new large airship, capable of flying day and night in all weathers between England and the major cities of the British Empire.

After much discussion, the new Labour government finally approved a proposal for the design and construction of *two* such airships: the R.100 ('R' for 'rigid') by a subsidiary of Vickers, headed by Burney, at Howden in Yorkshire; and the R.101 by the Air Ministry's Royal Airship Works at Cardington, near Bedford. This three-year project would involve a total investment in airships, mooring masts and airbases of £1.4 million[5] (**£60 million in 2007 pounds**). It would end with a flight to Karachi in January 1927.

The competition between R.100 and R.101

Rather than the cooperation that had been hoped for, the 'competition' between private enterprise (Vickers) and the Air Ministry produced plenty of unfriendly rivalry. The two airships' chief designers (Barnes Wallis and Richmond) never visited the other's works, nor did they meet or correspond about

4   Official inquiry: *R.101: The Airship Disaster, 1930*, Cd. 3825, HMSO, London, 1999, pp. 18–19.

5   Ibid., p. 15.

their common problems.[6] In fact they and their staffs had very different views.

R.100 was largely conventional in design, following Zeppelin practice in its general principles; while R.101 was a radical departure, with many innovations. The Royal Airship Works staff at Cardington felt they were working on research and development of national importance, too great to entrust to commercial interests. The Vickers staff disagreed. From 1916, after bitter experience, all construction of *aeroplanes* had been left to private enterprise. Not so for *airships*, where the 1921 disaster to the government-designed R38 (which killed 44 people) was still fresh in the memory.

The 700-foot-long R38, costing £500,000 (**£15 million**), had been intended for sale to the US Navy. In building it, there had been no attempt to calculate the aerodynamic forces acting on the ship in motion. On her fourth flight, while she was doing turning trials over the Humber in perfect weather, the airship had broken in two. The front part caught fire and fell in the river and the rear part came down on land. Now the same Cardington team, except one who had died in R38, would construct R.101 to compete with the Vickers R.100.

R.100 and R.101 were nearly twice as large as anything built before in the UK and more than one third again as large as the *Graf Zeppelin* (see Table 1). Moreover, their diameter was 'thicker' relative to length (the length/diameter ratio was lower). The requirements for the two new airships were exactly the same. Their size would be 5 million cubic feet. Their full speed was to be not less than 70 mph and the cruising speed 63 mph, with room for 100 passengers. The structure weight, including plant but

---

6   Nevil Shute, *Slide Rule*, Heinemann, London, 1954, p. 58.

excluding fuel, was not to exceed 90 tons, giving a useful lift of 60 tons. In the event, R.101 achieved neither the weight nor the speed requirements.[7]

Table 1 **Size of large airships**

Name of airship	Length(L) (feet)	Diameter (D) (feet)	L over D	Capacity (million cu. ft)
R38	695	86	8.1	2.7
Graf Zeppelin	777	100	7.8	3.7
R.100	709	133	5.3	5.0
R.101A*	732	132	5.5	5.0
R.101C	777	132	5.9	5.5

* The labels A, B and C denote R.101's three periods out of the hangar: R.101A, 12 October–30 November 1929; R.101B, 23–29 June 1930; R.101C, 1–5 October 1930.

The R.100 contract was for a fixed price (£350,000 [**£15 million**]), as was usual in those days.[8] It soon became obvious that Vickers would make a loss on the airship, so money was short. Excluding hand tools, Howden employed less than a dozen machines. Nevil Shute[9] says that a tale went round at Cardington to the effect that R.100 was getting on rather more quickly now that one of the Vickers staff had bought a car and lent its toolkit to the workshops!

Vickers could not afford much experimental work but could make rapid design changes if need be. For example, the company varied its engine policy three times. At first it seemed sensible

7   Official inquiry, op. cit., p. 16.

8   But between 1925 and 1930, prices in general were falling – that is, the purchasing power of money was actually *increasing*.

9   Shute, op. cit., p. 66. Nevil Shute (Norway), the novelist, was employed in 1924 as Chief Calculator on the R.100 at the age of 25 and by 1929 he was effectively second-in-command to Dennis Burney.

to design a special engine for R.100, running on hydrogen and kerosene; but a year's work showed that it would not be ready in time. The company then decided to fit diesel engines like those the Air Ministry was proposing for R.101. But after six months it was clear they would be grossly overweight and otherwise unsuitable. So then Vickers decided to use aeroplane engines running on petrol.

At Cardington things were different. They built a whole experimental section of R.101, at a cost of £40,000 (**£1.5 million**), and researched such things as gas valves, servo motors, steam heating of passenger quarters, and cooling of the engines. The Report of the Inquiry[10] commented: 'Originality and courage in design are not to be deprecated, but there is an obvious danger in giving too many separate hostages to fortune at one time.' So the way the two staffs worked provided a contrast. At Vickers they were frugal but flexible, while at Cardington they were more prodigal but also more bureaucratic and secretive.

As R.100's design progressed, Vickers had to submit every detail to the Air Ministry. They sent everything on to Cardington for independent comment, as was normal practice. It was different for the government airship. Two university professors did check the R.101's design, as to the strength of the main structure and the aerodynamic design. But other questions about the R.101 were never referred to anyone outside Cardington: for instance, with respect to fire hazard, outer cover defects, gas valve leakage, servo motors, astern power and engine defects.

R.100's useful lift was 6 tons (about 30 passengers), below the target of 60 tons (see Table 2). The total weight of R.101's power

10   Official inquiry, op. cit., p. 22.

installation was 17 tons, compared with 9 tons for R.100; though to cover 2,500 miles in still air, R.101 required only 17 tons of fuel oil versus R.100's 23 tons of petrol. Even so, the diesel engines weighed far more than expected, and the press highlighted the fact that the government airship was 25 tons overweight.

Table 2 **Weight details of R.100 and R.101**

(Tons)	Gross	Structure	Useful lift	Percentage
Target	150	90	60	40
R.100*	156	102	54	35
R.101A†	148	113	35	24
R.101B†	152	111	41	27
R.101C†	167	118	49	29

*Shute, op. cit., p. 79.   †Official inquiry, op. cit., p. 95.

R.101A and R.101B (Royal Airship Works)

R.101's extensive research work took two years, as did the process of erection in the huge shed at Cardington. After her launch, R.101A made seven separate flights lasting 70 hours in good weather without any full speed trial, including a 30-hour 'endurance flight'. But by late 1929 it became clear that R.101A was unable to carry enough fuel to fly to India. As a result it was decided to take out all unnecessary equipment (R.101B) and to insert a further section containing an extra gasbag in the middle of her length (R.101C). Altogether this would add 14 tons to the useful lift.

In June 1930, the modified R.101B came out for further trials, but did no full power trial. As soon as she was on the mast, in a very light wind, the outer cover split, making a tear 140 feet long. The next day there was a second shorter split. Both splits were repaired at once and extra tapes were stuck on inside to reinforce the cover.

The Cardington designers of R.101 were working to the same specification as R.100. But they had no contractual programme to satisfy, so flight trials were liable to be modified for public relations or political reasons. For example, R.101B's last two 'flight trials' involved her in the RAF rehearsal and display at Hendon in late June. At one point there was an unscheduled and dramatic fall to within 500 feet of the ground. During the two Hendon flights on successive days, each lasting for about twelve hours, she grew steadily heavier from loss of gas. This was probably caused by the gasbags chafing against the ship's girders: the wiring (rather like a net surrounding each gasbag) had been let out to increase the volume, which had resulted in many holes. After that, she did not fly again until after the insertion of the extra bay in late summer.

The inspector in charge of the Aircraft Inspection Department, Mr F. McWade, made a written report on R.101B's gas leaks on 3 July. He made a special point of sending his airworthiness report directly to the Secretary of the Air Ministry, marking it 'for the attention of the Director of Aeronautical Inspection' (Colonel Outram). He wrote:

> … This matter, in my opinion, has become very serious … Padding to the extent now necessary is, in my opinion, very unsatisfactory … I am fully aware that to remedy the faults complained of is in the nature of a large undertaking and it may be necessary to remove the bags from the ship. Until this matter is seriously taken in hand and remedied I cannot recommend to you the extension of the present 'Permit to Fly' or the issue of any further permit or certificate.[11]

---

11 Official inquiry, op. cit., pp. 72–3.

This was indeed a damning indictment.

Colonel Outram explained that he would have to pass Mr McWade's note on to Sir John Higgins, the Air Council member who dealt with such matters. Before he did so, however, he would like Cardington's comments. All the government's airship experts were working at Cardington: their 'superiors' at the Air Ministry in London mostly had experience only of aeroplanes, not airships. He was thus, in effect, asking R.101's designers to judge their own work. They replied that airship gasbags always had touched the girders and that a little padding of the girders was an effective cure preventing holes forming. This seemed to reassure Colonel Outram, who decided he need not trouble Sir John Higgins with Mr McWade's report on the gasbags after all.

In early June, Michael Rope, a senior designer at Cardington, was worried about the strength of the outer covers. He wrote: 'What scant information is available suggests that there is no margin of safety for flight in rough atmosphere. It is for consideration as to whether the risk involved in sending either ship on a long overseas flight is – or is not – greater than is justified by the need to fulfil public expectation.'[12] Here was another clear warning of potential disaster (which was not quoted at the official inquiry).

To reduce weight, R.101's engineers had initially used a new method: a 'pre-doped' cover, made of fabric that they had treated before stretching it around the structure. In the summer, however, alarmed by problems with the cover, they largely abandoned this idea. Instead, while the airship was being lengthened, they mostly replaced it with a new cover made of cotton and linen fabric,

---

12   Masefield, op. cit., p. 206.

which they would dope *after* fixing it to the ship. This had been the practice in earlier airships.

But the original outer cover remained in place in two main sections totalling 200 feet, just aft of the nose and around the fins at the tail. There they had used a rubber solution to attach a number of circular patches and some lengthwise reinforcing strips. Unfortunately wherever they had applied the rubber solution to the original cover, and not covered it with the patches or reinforcing strips, there had been serious damage to the fabric. It seemed the rubber solution reacted chemically with the dope. In parts it was friable, like scorched brown paper, so that if you crumpled it in your hand it broke up into flakes. So they stuck more strengthening bands along the length of the ship.

After R.101B's June trials the Cardington engineers began to put forward tentative proposals to postpone the 'demonstration flights' to the following year, on the grounds that at that stage neither ship was fit to make a long flight. But Vickers was keen to finish the competition. Winning it, and getting future airship contracts, would be their only chance of recouping the loss they had incurred on the R.100 fixed-price contract.

R.100 (Vickers)

The contract for R.100 required a final 48-hour acceptance trial followed by a demonstration flight to India. But when Vickers decided to equip her with petrol engines, the destination was changed to Canada. (In those days a flight to the tropics with petrol on board was thought too risky.) The final acceptance flight, in January 1930, lasted for 54 hours, with bad weather throughout. During the trial R.100 flew for several hours at 65 mph. The R.101's first officer, Noel Atherstone, who was on board, said: 'She handles better than R.101 and seems much lighter on the controls.'[13]

In all R.100 made seven flights before crossing the Atlantic. She had flown over 150 hours covering at least 7,000 miles, often at full speed and for long periods in very bad weather. The R.100's maximum speed was 81 mph (at least 10 mph more than the R.101), with a cruising speed of 70 mph. The engines were of a well-proved aeroplane type; though the six Rolls-Royce Condor IIIA engines, which Vickers had bought second-hand, were replaced by six more reliable new Condor IIIBs. But (as with R.101) there had been serious problems with the airship's outer covers.

Shute says: '… there is no doubt that our Atlantic crossing was dictated by political motives alone, as in the case of the Indian flight of R.101'.[14] There was pressure to show that the substantial public spending on the new airship programme over the past five years had been a wise investment. In the event, R.100's demonstration flight at the end of July 1930 was successful, though not without problems over Canada. It took 78 hours westward, averaging 42 mph, with 5 tons of petrol left (out of 35 tons), and 56 hours eastward averaging 58 mph.

At that time only one aeroplane had ever made a direct flight across the Atlantic from east to west against the prevailing wind. So R.100's performance, at twice the speed of any other form of transport from London to Montreal, suggested commercial promise; although she had been carrying only seven passengers. Moreover it had impressed the Americans, who were thinking about an airship mail service between the United States and Great Britain.

---

13   Ibid., p. 189.
14   Shute, op. cit., p. 109.

R.101C (lengthened): flight trials

R.100's successful flight to Canada at the end of July put all the pressure on to the Cardington team. They now had to fly R.101C to India or admit defeat in the competition. Captain Irwin had drawn up a programme of flight trials.[15] R.101C was to finish with 'a flight of 48 hours' duration under adverse weather conditions to windward of base. Ship to be flown for at least 6 hours continuous full-speed through bumpy conditions and the rest of the flight at cruising speed. Ship to be berthed in shed as soon after landing to mast as possible, and a complete bow to stern inspection carried out'. When R.101C had completed that trial successfully, he (and Sir John Higgins) would be satisfied. In their view, the airship would then be able to undertake the demonstration flight to India with only a moderate degree of risk. On 1 September 1930, Air Vice-Marshal Dowding replaced Sir John Higgins as Air Member for Supply and Research at the Air Ministry. At that time Dowding had never even been up in an airship.

On Wednesday, 1 October 1930, the giant airship emerged from the shed and on to the mooring mast. On that day and the next there was a trial flight of seventeen hours in dead calm conditions – only one third of what Captain Irwin had programmed.[16] (They had reduced the duration of the flight trial to 24 hours, in order for the airship to leave for India earlier; but in the event it had to be cut even shorter to enable Dowding, who was on board, to get to a meeting.) Once the airship left the mast, one engine's oil cooler failed so no full-power trial was possible. The loads on the outer cover increase as the *square* of the speed;[17] so a (full) speed of

---

15   Official inquiry, op. cit., p. 104.

16   Ibid., p. 95.

17   Masefield, op. cit., pp. 305, 313.

63 mph would have *doubled* the loads on the cover compared with the 44 mph of the final trial flight.

R.101C: pre-take-off

No airship had ever flown to India and back before. As early as November 1929 it had been announced that the end of September 1930 would be a suitable time for R.101 to attempt it. This was more than three and a half years later than the original schedule. In July 1930 Lord Thomson minuted: 'So long as R.101 is ready to go to India by the last week in September this further delay in getting her altered[18] may pass. I must insist on the programme for the Indian flight being adhered to, as I have made my plans accordingly.'[19]

Eventually it was arranged that R.101C would leave for India (via Egypt) at the beginning of October. She would aim to arrive back in England in time for Lord Thomson to appear at the Imperial Conference on 20 October. This was plainly going to be the most difficult flight that any British airship had ever made. It would be in an experimental airship that in its lengthened form had never flown at full power, or under adverse weather conditions, and which had also been suffering from serious gasbag and cover defects. Quite apart from all the technical problems, the crew of the R.101C had flown only for a few hours together. Moreover, her officers and crew, some of whom had been on almost constant duty for the previous fortnight, went aboard exhausted.

It is fair to recall that at the very beginning the airship programme was described as being for 'Government Research,

---

18   Waiting for R.100 to complete her flight to Canada.
19   Official inquiry, op. cit., p. 78.

Experiment and Development'. On 3 June 1930 Lord Thomson said in the House of Lords: 'These airships are still scientific experiments. They will not cease to be experimental until their overseas tests have been completed.'

But he may have been downplaying the risks. Despite Michael Rope's concerns, nearly everyone seems to have been confident about R.101's flight to India, both at Cardington and at the Air Ministry. On 27 June Lord Thomson said he was looking forward to going to India in R.101, adding: 'It is, of course, no particular adventure.' And he went on to quote a Zeppelin expert who had said of the airship: 'This is the safest conveyance on land, sea, or in the air that human ingenuity has yet devised.' But the R.101 was very different from any previous airship.

Lord Thomson held a final conference at the Air Ministry on Thursday, 2 October. He wanted to set off the following day, but the staff protested that the crew must have some rest. It was finally agreed to start for India on the evening of Saturday, 4 October. Towards the end of this conference (according to Dowding) Lord Thomson said: 'You must not allow my natural impatience or anxiety to start to influence you in any way. You must use your considered judgement.'[20] But nobody was likely to take him up on these fine words.

R.101C was to carry six passengers, including Lord Thomson and his valet, and six senior officials from the Royal Airship Works at Cardington. In addition there were five ship's officers and 37 crew – a total of 54 people. The 37 crew members' luggage weighed 468lbs; that of the other five passengers, six Cardington officials and five ship's officers weighed 492lbs. Lord Thomson's

---

20   Ibid., p. 105.

own luggage,[21] including a large carpet roll (129lbs) and two cases of champagne (52lbs), weighed no less than 254lbs. This seems extremely heavy, given that (as he must have known) weight was such a problem. Tom Cave-Browne-Cave, in charge of R.101's power-plant installations, always regarded the carpet as 'the last straw': he stayed behind to press on with engine development for R.102 (a planned successor airship of 7.5 million cubic feet).

Amazingly enough, there was even a question about who was in command of R.101C. Major Herbert Scott was in charge of flying and training for both airships at the Royal Airship Works. Captain Irwin of R.101 and Captain Booth of R.100 both reported to him at Cardington. But there was concern about possible problems if there was any conflict between Scott and the airship captain. Sir John Higgins had ruled[22] that on the demonstration flights of both R.100 and R.101 the captains must have full responsibility, and that Major Scott merely had the role of 'a non-executive Admiral'. Scott could give *advice* to the captain, who was not bound to take it.

But Major Scott was reluctant to delegate to the captains of the ships. He came on board the R.101 in uniform, despite travelling as an 'official passenger' from the Royal Airship Works, not as a 'ship's officer'. In fact Scott denied that he was a passenger: he continued to regard himself as being in charge of the demonstration flight to India (as he had on R.100's flight to Canada). He would decide such things as departure time, course, speed and height, while Captain Irwin commanded the crew. This was important because Scott was renowned for 'getting on with it', while Irwin was more cautious. Scott had also made several

---

21   Masefield, op. cit., pp. 479–80.

22   Ibid., pp. 241–2.

mistakes during R.100's and R.101's trial flights,[23] and his judgement had become increasingly dubious.

The increased length and capacity and the extra power had changed all R.101's control characteristics. So two experts were asked to report on R.101C with the extra bay, and the Air Council had said their report would guide them in deciding whether or not to certify R.101C as airworthy. (This is needed before an aircraft may fly over foreign territory.) Professor Bairstow wrote to the Air Ministry on 1 October: '… The difference between the conditions of loading of R.101 now submitted and those of the original design on which our previous report was based, surprised us by their magnitude … We have not had time … to prepare a sufficiently considered written report.'[24] In the event, they never completed it: the two professors were still working on their report when they received news of the disaster.

As soon as the inspectors were content with the ship's physical condition, someone in the Air Ministry wrote out the Certificate of Airworthiness. It was handed to R.101's captain just before the start of the flight to India. In fact, R.101C – as lengthened and modified – was virtually a new airship and really ought to have flown a complete series of test flights before getting its certificate.

The inquiry report noted: '… it is impossible to overlook the fact that the trials of the reconstructed ship were cut down to a degree that would never have been thought proper if it had not been for exigencies of time'.[25] The prime minister, Ramsay MacDonald, had actually asked Lord Thomson the day before he

---

23 See Shute, op. cit., p. 120; and Masefield, op. cit., pp. 62, 129, 132, 133, 135, 146, 313.

24 Official inquiry, op. cit., p. 84.

25 Ibid., p. 102.

left if he *really* had to go.[26] It was a good question, since there was no real reason for Lord Thomson to be on R.101's flight to India at all. (He did not go to Canada with R.100, though he had originally planned to.) So the supposed 'exigencies of time' – the 'need' for R.101 to start its journey in time for Lord Thomson to be able to return to the Imperial Conference by 20 October – were entirely spurious.

R.101C: the last flight

R.101C started from Cardington on her last flight at 6.35 p.m. GMT[27] on the evening of Saturday, 4 October 1930. (There had been a 25-minute delay in starting the starboard forward engine.) She then spent another 45 minutes circling over Bedford before setting course for London. The weather forecast was not good, though it was not bad enough for whoever was in charge to postpone departure. (Airships had to show they were not just fair-weather craft.)

But bad weather developed more quickly than expected. At 8.08 p.m. a later report was wirelessed to R.101, which was then over London. It forecast a wind over northern France of 40 to 50 mph, becoming more of a headwind, with much low cloud and rain. Ninety minutes out, it would have been perfectly possible to abandon the flight. R.101 could have returned to the mooring mast at Cardington to wait for better weather conditions. But it was decided to keep going.

With the increasing headwind, R.101 crossed the Channel

---

26   Masefield, op. cit., p. 322.

27   The local time was 7.35 p.m. British Summer Time. Clocks reverted to Greenwich Mean Time at 02.00 the next morning.

slowly. One engine went out of action for more than two and a half hours after 8 p.m.; it was not operational again until shortly before reaching the coast of France at about 11 p.m. To battle against the wind the airship then cruised on all five engines at a speed of 63 mph. R.101 had probably never before flown at such a high speed. She was, in effect, doing her full-power trial in extremely bad weather, in the middle of the night, over a foreign country.

By two in the morning, after flying for seven and a half hours, she had got only as far as Beauvais, 220 miles from Cardington. She was flying at about a thousand feet above the ground and nothing unusual had occurred so far. The watch was changed at 2 a.m. as normal, which suggests there was no sense of emergency. At every change of watch, the relieving coxswains needed about ten minutes to get the feel of the ship.

Just after two o'clock the ship got into a long and rather steep dive. She was brought out of this dive on to an even keel for a few moments. But then she dived again and at about 02.09 hit the ground, not very hard, nose first. That of itself need not have been disastrous: other airships had hit the ground without any serious consequences.[28] The official inquiry said: 'the disaster was caused by a substantial loss of gas in very bumpy weather'.[29] But Lord Brabazon, one of the assessors, candidly remarked years later: 'We never did find out why R.101 crashed.'[30]

Masefield says the reason for R.101 hitting the ground was that a split developed in the forward upper part of the outer cover, at the most highly stressed place of all: the section where they had not re-covered the original cover but merely reinforced it by

---

28   See Shute, op. cit., p. 90.

29   Official inquiry, op. cit., p. 154.

30   Masefield, op. cit., p. 11.

sticking on fabric bands. The decision to throttle back the engines (rather than *increase* power and go for height) then led to the nose dropping.

The inquiry suggested the cause of the fire was a spark from a broken electric circuit igniting a mixture of air and hydrogen gas escaping from the damaged gasbags. But there was a rack of calcium flares in the control car, right below the passenger berths. These flares ignited instantly on contact with water: some had been used to obtain drift sights over the English Channel. When the control car hit the ground in the very wet undergrowth near Beauvais, Masefield suggests, the calcium flares broke open and ignited.

As soon as R.101 hit the ground she burst into flames. A fierce fire spread from the centre of the airship to the gasbags above – and then fore and aft until it engulfed the whole airship. In a few seconds the airship was totally consumed. Of the 54 persons on board, only six survived, of whom four were engineers in the power cars. All the ship's officers, all the officials and all the passengers perished in the fire, including Lord Thomson.

Conclusion

Following the R.101 disaster in October, the R.100 never flew again. Naturally this was a great disappointment for the Howden team, which, after all, had 'won' the six-year competition between private enterprise (R.100) and government (R.101). Over its whole life, R.100 flew for 276 hours covering 11,134 nautical miles; while R.101 flew for 111 hours, covering 3,665 nautical miles.[31]

---

31   Ibid., p. 504.

Viscount Templewood (formerly Sir Samuel Hoare) wrote afterwards:

> The outstanding lesson left on my mind by this tragic
> calamity was the difficulty of carrying out a protracted
> and highly scientific programme ... in the full blaze of
> Parliamentary criticism. It would have been better to have left
> a plan that contained so many risks to private enterprise ...
> If the original plan [of six privately built airships] had been
> maintained, the loss of a single airship would not have meant
> the complete abandonment of the whole programme ...[32]

The airships were supposed to be able to accommodate 100 passengers each, but owing to the weight problems,[33] the maximum number over 1,500 miles or more was only 25. Both the R.100 and the R.101 had serious problems with the outer covers, which were never completely resolved. And Mr McWade's serious criticisms about the R.101's gasbags were never referred to Sir John Higgins. But another year or two (at modest extra cost) should have enabled both R.100 and R.101 to improve – if not completely overcome – their structural problems.

For the future it seemed that either the stopping places would need to be closer together, or the airships would need to be larger still, or both. Even so, serious problems with airships would still have remained: their need to fly low to conserve gas, in possible turbulence over land; their slow speed and vulnerability to adverse winds, which made reasonable punctuality impossible; their vast structures and mooring problems.

The original estimate in 1924 of the total cost for a three-year

---

32   Viscount Templewood, op. cit., p. 231.
33   At five passengers to the ton, a shortfall of 10 tons costs 50 passengers.

programme was £1.4 million (**£60 million**). The final cost[34] for a six-and-a-half-year programme was £2.4 million (**£100 million**), of which about half was on the airships themselves, the rest on the mooring masts, sheds and overseas bases. The R.100 ended up costing £470,000 (**£20 million**), the R.101 £710,000 (**£30 million**). The mooring masts at Ismailia and Karachi, which cost **£4.5 million**, were never used at all.

There were clearly problems during the R.101's last flight. There was reluctance to postpone the flight given a bad weather forecast, or to turn back when the weather got worse. When the airship suddenly lost height over northern France, it was decided to throttle back the engines instead of increasing power and going for height. But even if these decisions (with hindsight) are regarded as 'mistakes', they should not have been fatal. Carrying calcium flares in the control car below the passenger berths was perhaps more critical, since it may have led to immediate fire when the airship crashed.

Far more serious was the political pressure that led to blatant failure to complete Captain Irwin's required 48-hour flight trials for R.101 before the demonstration flight to India, including at least six hours of continuous full speed through bumpy weather conditions. Seventeen hours in fine weather with no full-speed trial was totally inadequate. In those circumstances it was irresponsible for the Air Ministry to issue a Certificate of Airworthiness.

---

34   Masefield, op. cit., pp. 484–5.

3 THE GROUNDNUT SCHEME (1946–54)

Background

Just after World War II, the British Empire reached its greatest extent.[1] It included the United Nations Trust territory of Tanganyika, formerly German East Africa, containing about 6 million Africans and 16,000 Europeans. (The population of Tanzania in 2007 is about 40 million.) The country covered 350,000 square miles, nearly seven times the area of England. Water supplies were scarce and people occupied only one sixth of the land area, because tsetse fly infested the rest.

From October 1946, Arthur Creech Jones was Secretary of State for the Colonies in the Labour government under Clement Attlee. His policy was to fund new central bodies to contribute to colonial development, one of them being the Overseas Food Corporation (OFC), to promote the bulk buying of staple crops. The Colonial Office's civil service staff numbers increased from 450 people in 1939 to 1,139 in 1947 and to 1,661 in 1954. Indeed, it became a paradigm case for Parkinson's 'law'[2] of bureaucratic expansion.

Frank Samuel was managing director of the United Africa

---

1   India and Pakistan (then including Bangladesh) became independent in August 1947.
2   C. Northcote Parkinson, *Parkinson's Law*, Penguin, Harmondsworth, 1957/1986, p. 22.

Company (UAC), a subsidiary of Unilever. Early in 1946 he visited Tanganyika, where only a small proportion of the land was under cultivation. He met R. W. R. Miller, Tanganyika's Director of Agricultural Production, who suggested growing groundnuts (peanuts). This annual crop is planted in East Africa when the rains begin in November and harvested four months later. Nearly half the kernel emerges as edible oil and the rest makes a cattle-feeding cake. Both men knew that Unilever would be keen to buy cheap nuts as a raw material for margarine.

Miller suggested planting at least 100,000 acres. He felt the economic success of any such scheme would depend upon it being entirely mechanised. Samuel doubted that backward natives, using only primitive hand tools, would be able to produce on such a scale. Their use of fire to clear the bush also led to serious erosion of the soil. But Samuel soon came to believe that 100,000 acres was far too little, and his view was that only a government enterprise would be able to clear and plant the huge area he had in mind. Moreover, conceding rights in large areas of Africa to private enterprises would be open to criticism.

The Wakefield Report

Meanwhile in London the government was in trouble over the low fats ration (food rationing in the UK after the war was even more restrictive than during it), so the Minister of Food, Sir Ben Smith, was keen to explore the prospects of groundnut production. Soon a mission went out, under John Wakefield, to look into Samuel's idea. Wakefield himself had worked in Tanganyika for eighteen years, ending as Director of Agriculture. With him were David Martin, UAC's plantations manager, and John Rosa, a banker

65

working in the Colonial Office. They spent nine weeks viewing potential terrain (mainly from the air) and finished their report by mid-September.

The Wakefield Report[3] proposed a large-scale project to establish 107 mechanised units, each of 30,000 acres: 80 in Tanganyika, 17 in Northern Rhodesia (now Zambia) and 10 in Kenya. The total would be 3,210,000 acres or just over 5,000 square miles – about six times the area enclosed by the M25 motorway round London. The British government would lease the land for 25 years from the local governments and there would be villages to house the workers. Eventually the undertakings would be transferred to the government concerned.

The preface to the report said: 'We are confident that the project … is a practicable one.' If the project started in 1947, within five years it could produce 600,000 tons of groundnuts a year. '[This] represents only a relatively small part of the present total shortfall of vegetable oils and fats, but we have no doubt that, given the will, this target figure could be *vastly exceeded* in course of time' (emphasis added). Mention of *time* draws attention to the ambition of trying to do in a short time what one would normally expect to take a generation or more.

Table 3 shows the suggested clearing and planting programmes on the basis of 850lbs of shelled nuts per acre. There would be a four-year rotation: two years of groundnuts alternating with two years of grass or with one year of grass and one year of another crop. The area planted in November/December 1947 would not be harvested until April/May 1948.

---

3   Cmd. 7030: *A Plan for the Mechanized Production of Groundnuts in East and Central Africa*, HMSO, London, February 1947 (pp. 11–48 comprising the Wakefield Report itself).

Table 3 **Wakefield's suggested annual programmes**

Year	Cleared each year '000 acres	Under groundnuts* '000 acres	Production '000 tonnes
1947	150	150	–
1948	450	600	57
1949	855	1,230	228
1950	855	1,605	467
1951	525	1,605	610
1952	375	1,605	610
Total	3,210		

*Cmd. 7030: *A Plan for the Mechanized Production of Groundnuts in East and Central Africa*, HMSO, London, February 1947, p. 22.

The report suggested that 'the establishment of the project would be accelerated if firms already equipped with the necessary machinery were engaged on contract for the initial land clearing'. But no such machines existed. Bush-clearing would eliminate the tsetse fly from a large area: it would employ 25,000 Africans at the peak, in 1949 and 1950, and 500 Europeans. Permanent farming would require 300 Africans per unit and about 750 Europeans in total.

Total capital spending of £24 million (**£600 million** in 2007 pounds) would cover six years: nearly £5 million for agricultural machinery, and the balance for land clearing and installations. Costs of production would be £14.30 per ton of shelled nuts. The current cost of purchasing groundnuts in the free market was £32.00 per ton ('a level likely to be maintained for several years') – which would leave a margin of about £17.00. With an annual crop of 600,000 tons,[4] that would mean a saving of more than

4   850lbs per acre x 30,000 acres = 25.5 million lbs per unit = 11,400 tons; 11,400 tons x 107 units = 1,220,000 tons /2 = 610,000 tons in total in any year.

£10 million (**£250 million**) a year in Britain's food bill.

The report said areas of sparse population, unencumbered by native or other rights, were needed to enable operations to start quickly. It suggested that: '*Uninhabited, tsetse-infected and waterless areas therefore offer special attraction to the project*, provided the soil is suitable and rainfall adequate …' (emphasis added). Wakefield believed the main reason for Tanganyika's apparent barrenness was local primitive farming practices that Western equipment could overcome.

The summary said: 'The rainfall in all the localities selected for the project is adequate for the groundnut crop … There is an abundance of additional land suitable for an extension of the production …'[5] A special section in the Ministry of Food broadly endorsed Wakefield's conclusions, but reduced the likely average yield from 850 to 750lbs per acre. But the basis for such yields was unreliable samples from selected localities. It was simplistic to extrapolate them across large areas as if land were a homogeneous factor of production.

Wakefield recommended an extensive scientific research programme for the first two years, covering meteorology, soil fertility studies, soil surveys and mapping, crop disease surveys and variety testing. But this research was to *follow*, not precede, the confident proposal for growing groundnuts on a vast scale. It seems not to have occurred to anyone that the research might result in new knowledge, calling for fundamental changes in the whole scheme.

---

5   Cmd. 7030, op. cit., p. 17, paras 16 and 18.

Government

In October 1946, less than six weeks after the Wakefield Report, the Labour government ('recognising the urgency') decided to proceed. The White Paper said: 'the scheme is a practicable plan … it is agriculturally sound … it involves no unjustifiable financial risk'. [6] The maximum cash requirement for the scheme was unlikely to exceed £23 million, allowing for proceeds from the sale of crops. Another £2.5 million would be required for railway, port and road construction.

Edith Penrose[7] was enthusiastic. She called it: 'A great African project – an imaginative attempt to develop an extremely backward area of the world – which would more than double the total value of Tanganyika's exports.' She wrote: 'There are large numbers of people [in America and elsewhere] who apparently believe that all colonial policy is "imperialist" in some vague sense and therefore sinister. The chief difference between modern colonial policy and older imperialism is the emphasis in the former on the importance for its own sake of the social, economic and political development of the native peoples.' Clearly this appealed to Creech Jones and his cabinet colleagues. They wanted the groundnut scheme to show the natives what could be done.

'By far the most important long-term advantage of the scheme from the African point of view is … the revolution in agricultural technique which it represents.'[8] But a mechanised project on such a large scale meant a complete reversal of the policy of preserving native ways of life as much as possible (rather like *Star Trek*'s 'Prime Directive'). It would involve moving a huge

---

6   Ibid., p. 4.

7   Edith T. Penrose, 'A great African project', *Scientific Monthly*, April 1948, pp. 322–6.

8   Cmd. 7030, op. cit., p. 6.

fleet of tractors to East Africa; providing workshops to maintain them; and building roads, railways and ports to supply them. In a country with almost no industry, this was a massive task, not to be embarked on lightly. Indeed, as Alan Wood pointed out: '... they were proposing a colossal engineering and agricultural revolution, something comparable on a small scale to the Russian Five-Year Plans, *without even realizing what they were doing*'.[9]

Apparently it was felt that the Colonial Office was ill equipped to run such a vast enterprise – so the Ministry of Food was asked to manage the groundnut scheme. Being in charge of rationing at home, everything they did was bound to be high-profile. (In contrast, a modest proposal by the Colonial Office might have attracted much less attention.) The choice of a different ministry was also a recipe for friction, both in London and in East Africa.

The cabinet decided that a government corporation should manage the scheme rather than private enterprise. But the new Minister of Food, John Strachey, an old Etonian ex-Marxist, was in a hurry, claiming that 'time was of the essence'. So he chose not to start with a pilot scheme, as Lord Huntingdon, then a junior agriculture minister, suggested. Instead he asked Frank Samuel's UAC to get things going straight away. They undertook this work on a cost-only basis. UAC's general manager on the spot was David Martin, a member of the Wakefield mission.

Whatever the minister's own impatience (he was not a member of the cabinet), it seems astonishing that nobody else in government urged starting the scheme on a much smaller scale. Attlee's obituary of Strachey in 1963 said: 'Looking back on it, I think his only mistake was to go in on a large scale, instead of

9   Alan Wood, *The Ground Nut Affair*, Bodley Head, London, 1950, p. 46.

starting with a pilot scheme.' A 1953 critic[10] noted that before work began at Kongwa, there was no time for sustained primary reconnaissance and survey, for photographic work, for soil maps, for adequate inquiry into rainfall data, or even for an adequate review of the economic aspects of crop yields.

Location

The scheme never got going at all in Northern Rhodesia or Kenya. In Tanganyika there were to be three groundnut areas:

- 15 units (of 30,000 acres each) at Kongwa in Central Province, 240 miles inland from Dar es Salaam, near the Central Railway Line. It was hot and dusty, with thick bush and baobab trees, and rainfall was erratic.
- 10 units at Urambo in Western Province, a further 300 miles west along the Central Railway Line. The rainfall was higher than at Kongwa, and there were tall trees fairly close together. The region was infested with tsetse fly.
- 55 units at Nachingwea in the more fertile Southern Province, 200 miles south of Dar es Salaam and 100 miles inland. During the rainy season the area was cut off from the rest of the country and the coast road to Dar was impassable. There was no railway until the end of 1949. The road was very poor in places. The region was infested with tsetse, and there was a lack of water.

10   S. Herbert Frankel, 'The Kongwa experiment: lessons of the East African groundnut scheme', in *The Economic Impact of Under-developed Societies*, Cambridge, MA, 1953, p. 146.

It was decided to establish the first unit in Central Province, with the first camp at Sagara, where there were few trees needing removal. This site had plenty of water, but it was difficult to take land without infringing African rights. An early survey showed that the ground was deficient in phosphates and nitrates. There was also much more clay than in the main US regions that had tried mechanised production of groundnuts. Moreover, the ground comprised mostly quartz sand with crystals as hard as steel.

Following the survey they moved the camp nearer Kongwa, a small native village comprising a few mud houses. This was seven miles from the units where the groundnut clearing would begin, but closer to the new branch railway from the central railway line from Dar es Salaam to Dodoma. Fresh water had to be brought in by truck. The surveyor, Dr Hugh Bunting,[11] head of the Scientific Department, thought rainfall would be adequate, but noted: 'Actual rainfall figures for the area are entirely lacking ...' Apparently local people referred to Kongwa as 'the country of perpetual drought'.[12]

Clearing the ground

The first task was to hire contractors to clear the ground, a major problem which the Wakefield Report had hardly mentioned. UAC agreed a contract with Sir John Gibson, of Pauling & Co., on the basis of cost plus 22.5p per acre cleared.[13] This was later modified

---

11 The managing agency's first monthly report to the Ministry of Food included among the supplies delivered one slide rule handed to Dr Bunting!

12 John Iliffe, *A Modern History of Tanganyika*, Cambridge, 1979, p. 442.

13 The cost of clearing was expected to be under £4.00 per acre, on the basis of A. L. Gladwell's experience.

because it was hard to define what 'cleared' meant. Such a 'cost-plus' arrangement provided little incentive to keep costs down. At the same time, UAC recruited men to grow the groundnuts after Pauling's had cleared the ground. Many of the managers to run the 30,000-acre units were to come from UAC; but the field assistants were mostly young men from the army.

The next step was to find machines to do the clearing. In Canada David Martin placed an order with Massey-Ferguson and Unilever agents all over the world tried to get hold of second-hand tractors. The biggest find came from the Philippines, where the US Army had left behind huge stocks of bulldozers. As Wood[14] pointed out, in the early post-war days the bulldozer still had the glamour of its wartime exploits. A fleet of them could bash down bush, build roads and push aside all obstacles. But economics counted for little in wartime. The tractor, which had evolved in America with its high labour costs, was likely to be an extravagant way of doing things in low-wage Africa. As Frankel said: '... without a highly skilled industrial population to draw on – non-existent in Africa – the machine easily becomes a liability rather than an asset'.[15]

There were two big transport problems in 1947: the congested harbour at Dar es Salaam, which persisted until 1950, and the railway, which could not handle the increase in traffic. There were no deep-water berths to cope with freighters carrying machinery, so the heavy equipment had to be brought ashore in stages. Everything was unloaded and left piled up on the quayside, from tinned food and light bulbs to second-hand army surplus trousers and generators. It was chaos.

14   Alan Wood, op. cit., p. 47.
15   Frankel, op. cit., p. 148.

The tractors required 40,000 gallons of diesel fuel per week, but the central railway line could carry only 22,000 gallons. So during much of the first year the tractors could be used only for two and a half days a week. Many of them were frequently out of action anyway, owing partly to lack of competent drivers and partly to lack of spare parts. The rail link to Kongwa from the central railway line was still incomplete, so this distance (about twenty miles) had to be covered by road.

The Wakefield Report's target was 200 tractors on-site by February to clear 150,000 acres in 1947. But that winter's great freeze-up stranded the tractors in Britain. Sixteen reached Dar es Salaam at the beginning of April. By the end of August, the 200 tractors had arrived on-site at Kongwa; but most of them had broken down and the whole fleet had to be brought in for overhaul in the Heavy Repair Workshop.

Preparing the ground involved three stages: clearing the scrub by flattening the bush; using bulldozers to move the bush and establish windrows to prevent soil erosion; and clearing the roots left behind in the soil. Two bulldozers linked by a strong chain could cut a swathe through the bush; but someone in London cancelled an order for ship anchor chains, not understanding their purpose. The third stage proved difficult. The firm of Blaw Knox had to design a new tool: rooters with special horizontal blades to cut the roots going straight down, and vertical discs to cut the lateral roots. But these were too late for the first year.

Even when the tractors were there in working order, local conditions were very difficult. For example, large baobab trees were hard to remove. One of them was a local tribal jail, another was a site of ancestor worship, and many had bees' nests in their hollow trunks. Wood wrote: 'In patches the thickets of scrub are impenetrable. A rhinoceros can force a way through: a snake can wriggle through: but no size or shape of animal in between.'[16]

Labour

The groundnut scheme also had to train African workers from tribes that were still extremely primitive. Many of the early labour recruits had served with the King's African Rifles during the war. But after a few months back in their native villages they had forgotten all the mechanical skills learnt in army trades. They found it difficult to cope with the machines brought in to plant the nuts. And the growing number of broken tractors led to the famous jest that the African worker's motto was: 'Give us the job and we will finish the tools!'[17]

There was very high labour turnover, which cost time in training new staff. But this training had no general value to the local economy. Despite the scheme's capital intensity, labour was a big problem, with several conflicts between labour and management. The Colonial Office sent two men to help the Africans form their own local trade union; but they promptly decided to go on strike in support of the dockworkers at Dar es Salaam.

Europeans had joined the project in the hope of soon becoming managers of 30,000-acre farms; but a year later they were still doing minor tasks and became unhappy. There were also problems with housing. Sir Ralph Furse, with long experience of selecting colonial administrators, wrote: 'Millions were wasted in the enthusiasm of ignorance, and by the employment on the spot of staff who had been hurriedly selected, who did not understand

16   Wood, op. cit., p. 64.
17   Parodying Churchill's wartime boast: 'Give us the tools and we will finish the job.'

the local conditions and who were too self-confident to take advice from those who did.'[18]

The first year

The essence of growing groundnuts is to clear the ground, plant the nuts and four months later dig them out again. For every nut inserted, the plant that grows from the original seed produces thirty or forty. Clearing the ground was extremely difficult. At Kongwa there was a short season of up to six weeks in which to complete planting. Temporary droughts during the growing season could cause significant crop losses; but the Wakefield mission was confident that adopting soil conservation measures and applying other principles of good farming could largely mitigate any ill-effects. Finally digging the nuts out after four months or so was also tricky.

For these operations many different machines were required. A tractor first ploughs the ground, then tows a planter with boxes of seed and fertiliser which gives rows of seeds at regular intervals. When the groundnuts come up mechanical diggers cut into the ground and bring the mature nuts to the surface. The side rake turns the nuts over to dry, and heaps them in long lines. Next the combine advances along the lines, picks the nuts up, separates them from the plant, and packs them neatly in sacks. For all these operations Massey-Harris had complex machines, but they were not well suited to the African bush.

When harvesting time first came at Kongwa, the diggers had been offloaded at Zanzibar and arrived only a month later.

---

18   Sir Ralph Furse, *Aucuparius: Recollections of a Recruiting Officer*, Oxford University Press, 1962, p. 304.

Unfortunately the stores and workshops were sited on an old lake-bed, so in the rainy season flash floods washed some of them away. After that the hot season baked the clay so solid that the digger-blades found it difficult to penetrate at all. Some of the nuts shattered and broke away from the plant. In the end there were still quite a number left behind in the soil. The crop gave an average yield less than half the revised estimate of 750lbs per acre.

By the end of 1947 it should already have been clear that there were serious flaws in the Wakefield Report's groundnut scheme. It had grossly underestimated the cost, since the scheme had to build roads, railways, airstrips and hospitals, and lay on water supplies and sanitation. It had also badly misjudged the transport and supply problems and the workshops needed for heavy tractors. It seemed that the report may have been wrong, too, in thinking that clearing was possible all the year round. Tests showed that results were much better in the wet season, when the roots came out cleanly.

In April 1947, Martin had been confident that the first year would see 150,000 acres (five 'units') under cultivation at Kongwa. By August UAC still had 'every reason to hope' they would plant 30,000 acres, but by the end of October they had managed to clear only 12,000 acres. The official report for the year finally said: '13,750 acres were cleared and 7,500 were planted'. But that was only 5 per cent of the plan.

The first progress report[19] in January 1948 said – incredibly! – that the first year's work had not revealed any basic faults in the scheme: 'There is no ... reason ... to doubt that the whole scheme – modified here and there as to its details – can be carried out on

19   Cmd. 7314, HMSO, London.

the broad lines and within the time schedule set out.' All that had happened, Strachey insisted, was that the scheme was a year late in getting going. The 7,500 acres planted amounted to a small-scale trial; 1948 would become Year 1 of the scheme, with its target of 150,000 acres.

Early in 1947 4,000 tons of groundnuts were ordered as seed for the first season's planting. Because they had cleared so little land, only a small fraction of these were planted. By mid-1949, the second season's harvest had produced about 2,000 tons of groundnuts (compared with 57,000 tons in the plan). So the output from the scheme after two years was actually *fewer* ground-nuts than there had been at the beginning!

But this negative result did not prompt those in charge to abandon the whole scheme. There was strong official resistance to this. Sir Frank Lee, Permanent Secretary at the Ministry of Food, wrote: 'Our standing as an imperial power in Africa is to a substantial extent tied up with the future of this scheme. To abandon it would be a humiliating blow to our prestige everywhere.'[20]

The Overseas Food Corporation

The government's Overseas Food Corporation (OFC) started early in 1948 with £50 million capital (**£1,250 million**) and took over the groundnut scheme from UAC in the spring. The change of management almost certainly delayed learning some of the lessons from the first year's work. Most of the new team knew nothing of agriculture or the tropics.

UAC waived their right to six months' notice, but refused

---

20   Rizzo Matteo, *The Groundnut Scheme Revisited*, Doctoral thesis, 2005.

liability for shortfalls in stocks totalling £330,000 (**£8 million**). The supplies seem to have been in a complete shambles. For the OFC's first financial year, the auditors said: 'We are unable to report that proper books of account have been kept ...'

The OFC's chairman was Leslie Plummer, a senior manager in Lord Beaverbrook's Daily Express newspaper group. His deputy, James McFadyen, was a director of the Co-operative Wholesale Society. Other full-time members of the board were: John Wakefield and John Rosa, both members of the original mission, and Sir Charles Lockhart, from the colonial civil service. Three part-time members were: Sir Frank Stockdale, a former agricultural adviser from the Colonial Office (who died in 1949); Lord Rothschild, the scientist; and Frank Samuel.

Strachey chose an army engineer, Major-General Desmond Harrison, to be the board's Resident Member in East Africa. He tried to run the scheme as a military operation. But he was unwell and stayed less than a year. At least the army provides a well-defined chain of command: every man knows what his own job is and how it fits into the general scheme. According to Alan Wood: 'These virtues were lacking at Kongwa, with an administrative structure of incredible complexity, and a general air of mystery in high places. Plans for future development were guarded as jealously as though they were military orders, where any breach of security would cost thousands of men's lives.'[21]

Decisions tended to be made in London, rather than locally, which often led to long delays. This was a serious drawback. Wood says: 'There were three separate areas [in Tanganyika], each a full-time job for one first-rate man on the spot. They could not

---

21   Wood, op. cit., p. 122.

possibly be run by one central control based on Kongwa, still less by a Board of Directors sitting in London.'[22]

There were cost-plus arrangements with different contracting firms to clear the ground at each site: Pauling's at Kongwa, Earth Moving & Construction, a company formed by A. L. Gladwell, at Urambo, and Mowlem's at Nachingwea. This did offer diversity, but in a matter where nobody had much relevant experience it also meant in effect reinventing the wheel. There were also frictions between the contractors and OFC staff.

How the original scheme turned out

In September 1948 Harrison returned to London with proposals for a revised plan: to clear 3.25 million acres in ten years rather than in six. After three years, instead of 1,600,000 acres under cultivation costing £24 million (£15 per acre), the new plan would have had 600,000 acres costing £48 million (£80 per acre). When Harrison had to retire because of ill health, it emerged that the new plan would cost £120 million (**£3,000 million**).

But Stafford Cripps, the Chancellor of the Exchequer, turned down the request to increase the OFC's £50 million capital. This meant it would be impossible to carry out even the original scheme, since the available funds would soon run out. His refusal to throw more good money after bad was one of the few signs of decent management in the whole affair. Even so the groundnut scheme cost about twice as much as had been predicted at the start.

This became public knowledge only in autumn 1949;

---

22 Ibid., p. 147.

meanwhile Strachey was still sounding optimistic. In March he suggested[23] that although the costs might be twice as high as the original estimate, so might the revenues – owing to an increase in the market price of groundnuts. He said: 'Today the only criticism we can make of those [initial] estimates is that they did not go far enough.' He claimed the scheme could generate the original savings from planting 'only' 2.0 million acres instead of 3.2 million. In November 1949 he dismissed Wakefield and Rosa from the OFC board.

Widespread drought struck Central and Western provinces in 1948 and 1949 and it became obvious that growing groundnuts at Kongwa or at Urambo was not going to work. So they reduced the target from fifteen and ten units respectively to 'only' six units (i.e. 180,000 acres!) in each of the two areas. Then the emphasis shifted to Nachingwea in the fertile Southern Province, which Wakefield had suggested as the place to start.

Indeed, it had been due to represent more than half the total acreage of the whole scheme: 1,650,000 acres. But Cmd. 8125 said that 'close examination of the agricultural potential of the area [revealed] that not more than 150,000 acres within an economic radius of Nachingwea could be made available for agriculture'. That was less than 10 per cent of the initial plan for the Southern Province.

After the February 1950 general election, Maurice Webb succeeded Strachey as Minister of Food. Later that year he told the cabinet: 'The original conception of the East African groundnuts scheme must be abandoned. There is no hope of the UK receiving any significant supply of oil-seeds from this scheme.' Doubtless

---

23   HoC Hansard, 14 March 1949, col. 1759.

this was the right decision, though rather a long time was taken to reach it. The White Paper[24] announcing the change of plan contained a forlorn sentence, tucked away in para. 11(B) of the Appendix: 'The groundnut is not a plant which lends itself readily to mass methods over vast acreages.' Hard-won knowledge!

The reduced project

In 1951 the OFC's functions were radically altered. Instead of 'large scale commercial production of groundnuts', the task became 'the investigation of the economics of clearing and mechanized agriculture under tropical conditions'. And the new scheme was to be under the Colonial Office. In all three areas they would farm in units of between 1,500 and 6,000 acres, rather than the initial idea of 30,000-acre farms. (They also tried other crops, such as sunflowers, as well as groundnuts.) But even this new, much smaller project had very disappointing results.[25]

At Kongwa the plan was to continue for three years cultivating the 12,000 acres under crop. The 1951/52 season was successful; in 1952/53 there was severe drought and the crops were almost a total failure; in 1953/54 rainfall was patchy. Uncertain rainfall in that area made any further investment too hazardous.

At Urambo they planted 40,000 acres in 1951. Despite an average season the yield was very disappointing, rosette disease severely damaging the groundnuts. In 1952/53 the results of planting only 250 acres of groundnuts were poor owing mainly to deficient rainfall. Instead it was hoped to grow flue-cured tobacco.

24   Cmd. 8125.
25   Cmd. 9158, 1954.

At Nachingwea the OFC proposed to substitute hand labour for part of the work machines were doing. This was a major change. The plan was to clear 15,000 acres a year for agricultural production. In 1951/52 16,000 acres were under cultivation. The cost of land-clearing exceeded the estimates while the crop revenue fell short of forecast. In the south they used 'Shervicks' – 175hp Sherman Mark III tanks converted by Vickers Armstrong. But these were underpowered, and four tanks in place of two tractors were needed; many of them soon broke down. So they concluded that there was no future for mechanised agriculture in the area.

A new rail line to Nachingwea opened in October 1949; but bottlenecks occurred all along the supply route. A new port was being developed at Mtwara in Southern Province, which, with the railway, would end up costing about £6 million. The OFC wrote off the £3.7 million it had spent up to April 1953.

From 1954 a new Tanganyika Agricultural Corporation (TAC) would carry on the OFC's current work and the OFC itself would be dissolved. The government had spent about £49 million in total (**£1,200 million**) on the groundnut scheme. Of this perhaps £3 million might represent the value of capital assets handed over to the TAC. Thus the net loss to the British taxpayer was about £46 million (**£1,150 million**).

Conclusion

The very concept of mechanisation (replacing cheap labour with expensive capital) was totally inappropriate for East Africa; the notion of economies of scale with such variable conditions over a wide area was misplaced; infrastructure requirements were grossly underestimated; and the failure to arrange for a pilot scheme was an extremely expensive mistake.

At a more down-to-earth level, there was inadequate data on rainfall, insufficient analysis of the soil and failure to appreciate the many problems in clearing the ground. For a large agricultural project these are rather serious shortcomings. A widespread scientific research programme was to *follow*, not precede, the large-scale implementation of the scheme.

Finally there was a costly delay of two years before the government admitted the plan was hopeless. This may have been genuine incompetence, but more likely it represented the minister's attempt to save face.

Overall this grandiose project was a complete fiasco, well deserving its place in our folk memory more than half a century later. The cost was large (**£1,150 million**) and it is hard to point to any offsetting benefit at all.

Acronyms

OFC	Overseas Food Corporation
TAC	Tanganyika Agricultural Corporation
UAC	United Africa Company

4 NUCLEAR POWER (1958–78– …)

Background

In the early post-war years, coal, gas and electricity were state-owned and governments also intervened extensively in oil. A major influence on policy was concern about a future 'energy gap'. Politicians and civil servants would estimate future energy consumption, deduct expected domestic coal production, and thus arrive at a 'gap' needing to be filled by other fuels. In free markets, of course, possibly after time lags, rising *prices* will normally tend to eliminate shortages, either by reducing demand or increasing supply or both.

On becoming prime minister again in 1951, Churchill was amazed to find that the post-war Attlee government had secretly spent nearly £100 million (**£2,500 million** in 2007 pounds) on atomic energy for military purposes.[1] Using the knowledge gained, it was in the 1950s that British governments first formed policies towards civilian uses of nuclear power. Coal, Britain's only important indigenous energy source at that time, began a continuing decline from its 1952 production peak of 230 million tonnes to only one tenth of that level today. Meanwhile consumption was increasing rapidly and nuclear power seemed to be a possible way to close the energy 'gap'. A small nuclear reactor was already under

---

1   Margaret Gowing, *Independence and Deterrence: Britain and Atomic Energy, 1945–52*, Macmillan, Basingstoke, 1974, 2 vols, vol. I, p. 406.

construction at Calder Hall, both to make plutonium (mainly for weapons) and to generate electricity.

The Atomic Energy Authority (AEA), formed in 1954, was responsible both for military and civilian uses of atomic power. It was keen to build commercial-scale power stations with the same 'Magnox' technology[2] as the existing small reactors. Alongside coal and oil, uranium was a third, non-fossil, fuel. But 'the complete burn-up of one tonne of natural uranium by fission would release as much energy as the burning of *three million* tonnes of coal'.[3] The 1951 takeover of British Petroleum's Persian oil operations increased supply fears, so policymakers were keen to diversify energy sources away from imported oil.

There were three separate AEA groups:

- Research, at Harwell, under Sir John Cockcroft
- Weapons research, at Aldermaston, under Sir William Penney
- Production, at Risley, under Sir Christopher Hinton.

The AEA advised the government and the supply industry on reactor types suitable to generate electricity. These scientists and engineers[4] knew far more about nuclear power than anyone else. They formed a powerful pressure group, able and willing to dazzle ministers and civil servants with science.

---

2   Magnox reactors used natural uranium sheathed in magnesium alloy as fuel, carbon dioxide as coolant, and graphite as a moderator for the nuclear reaction. For technical details explained for laymen, see Walter C. Patterson, *Nuclear Power*, Penguin, Harmondsworth, 1976, especially Part I, pp. 23–114.

3   Gowing, op. cit., vol. 2, p. 300.

4   In *The New Men* (Macmillan, Basingstoke, 1954, ch. XXV), C. P. Snow briefly distinguishes the respective attitudes of scientists and engineers.

The first nuclear power programme

In February 1955 the Churchill government decided on Britain's first civilian nuclear power programme, aiming to build twelve Magnox nuclear power stations by 1965. Total output would be between 1,500 and 2,000MW, just under 10 per cent of total existing capacity. Their capital cost would be £300 million[5] (**£5,500 million**). The White Paper reckoned that electricity from the first nuclear stations would cost 'about the same' as from new coal-fired stations; but that estimate was 'subject to a wide margin of uncertainty'. Among the variables were capital costs, fuel and running costs, useful life, load factor and decommissioning costs.

Within two years the first civil nuclear programme was *tripled* in size. By 1965 there were now to be 5,000–6,000MW of Magnox plant in twenty stations, at a capital cost of about £1,000 million[6] (**£17,000 million**). Two main factors were behind the huge increase. First, the Suez crisis exacerbated fears about the insecurity of oil supplies. In short, the Macmillan government panicked. Second, in 1956 Calder Hall became the first nuclear power station in the world to produce electricity for a grid system; hence nuclear power came to be regarded as a British technical triumph. Some scientists even claimed that Britain was the world leader in nuclear generating technology; but that claim related to high *volume* of output so far, not to low cost. From the beginning the Ministry of Fuel and Power strongly supported a nuclear power programme, 'above all' because it could contribute greatly to national prestige.[7]

5   Roger Williams, *The Nuclear Power Decisions, British Policies 1953–78,* Croom Helm, 1980, p. 64.

6   Duncan Burn, *The Political Economy of Nuclear Energy,* Research Monograph 9, IEA, London, 1967, p. 20.

7   Gowing, op. cit., vol. 2, p. 300.

For a while, there was great British optimism about future costs: in the AEA's famous boast, nuclear-generated electricity would soon become 'too cheap to meter'. One of the earliest forecasts was by Sir Christopher Hinton (later Lord Hinton), then AEA Member for Production and Engineering, and later chairman of the Central Electricity Generating Board (CEGB). He was a great driving force in the early development of nuclear power in Britain. Hinton prophesied[8] that by 1962 Magnox plants would probably have lower costs than coal plants, and that by 1970 nuclear costs would be 30 per cent lower. He suggested that by the late 1960s, three-quarters of new generating plant ordered in Britain might be nuclear.[9]

But the outcome was very different. By the early 1960s the 'shortages' of fossil fuels that post-war planners expected had turned into 'surpluses'. So fossil fuel prices fell. At the same time, nuclear costs rose sharply as Magnox plants overran on both time and cost, owing partly to faulty estimates and partly to design changes. As a result, the CEGB slightly reduced the Magnox programme in size (to 5,000MW) and extended it in time (to 1968).

Hinton himself pointed out[10] that 'from 1946 to 1954 atomic energy was a defence industry where speed was vitally necessary and great risk of failure had to be accepted'. As a result of those habits persisting, the industry was still taking uncomfortably high risks of technical failure. In 1959, Arthur Palmer, later chairman of the Select Committee on Science and Technology, feared that the

---

8 Sir Christopher Hinton, 'The future of nuclear power', *British Nuclear Energy Conference Journal*, July 1957, pp. 292–305.

9 Burn, op. cit., p. 21.

10 Sir Christopher Hinton, 'Nuclear power', *Three Banks Review*, December 1961, p. 5.

UK might be getting needlessly expensive electricity after investing 'too much, too hastily, in high-cost nuclear stations'.

In October 1957 a major fire broke out at Britain's infant nuclear reactor at Windscale, Cumbria. The resulting cloud of radioactive contamination (though small compared with Chernobyl in 1986) was much more life-threatening than the fallout from the 1979 meltdown at Three Mile Island. Only a summary was published of Sir William Penney's report, which found poor staff judgement and faulty instruments. But Harold Macmillan did warn de Gaulle about the Windscale accident, to alert him to the dangers that could arise in similar French reactors.

Safety was a major concern in the nuclear context, especially after the Windscale accident. The Nuclear Installations Inspectorate (NII) was set up in 1959 to advise on safety in all nuclear installations other than the AEA's small-scale experimental reactors, though it became fully separate from the AEA only on the creation of the Health and Safety Executive in 1975. The UK's health and safety record in the civil nuclear industry has been extremely good.[11] But there was no similar independent check on the nuclear establishment's 'experts' with respect to the *economics* of nuclear power.

In the end, the first nuclear power programme resulted in eight Magnox power stations in England and Wales and one in Scotland, with a total capacity of 3,800MW. There were numerous technical problems both in building and in operation: in the late 1960s corrosion and vibration problems reduced the output of most reactors. Thus the outcome was about 25 per cent less than the revised plan for 5,000MW by 1968. The average

---

11   Williams, op. cit., p. 263.

station size rose sharply from 150MW at first to 425MW in the final outcome.

In 1954 five consortia were formed to build nuclear plant, each comprising a heavy electrical plant manufacturer and a boiler-maker. Nearly every station was of slightly different design and the absence of replication proved expensive. But there was never really enough work for so many different groupings, and as the size of the stations grew larger, fewer were needed. So the five consortia became three, then two and finally, from 1973, one. But the consortia were always the poor relations in dealing with the CEGB monopsony.

Table 4 **The first nuclear programme's stations**

First nuclear programme: 5,000–6,000MW	Actual net output MW	Consortium
Berkeley	280	Nuclear Energy Co. Ltd
Bradwell	250	Nuclear Power Plant Co. Ltd
Hunterston A*	300	GEC-Simon-Carves
Trawsfynydd	390	Atomic Power Constructions
Dungeness A	420	Nuclear Power Plant Co. Ltd
Sizewell A	420	Atomic Power Group
Hinkley Point A	470	Atomic Power Group
Oldbury	430	Nuclear Power Plant Co. Ltd
Wylfa	840	Atomic Power Group
Total	3,800	

* South of Scotland Electricity Board (SSEB): all others for CEGB.

The nuclear stations, far from being cheaper, produced electricity at a cost about *twice* as high as coal-fired stations.[12] But it did seem that the Magnox stations might have longer lives than

12   Burn, op. cit., p. 21.

the assumed fifteen to twenty years. Estimating the incremental costs of nuclear power stations is not easy. They have very high capital costs, but low running costs, whereas coal-fired stations are the other way round. It is the incremental cost of running the whole system which matters. Once nuclear power stations have been built, it pays to operate them ahead of coal-fired stations in the grid's 'merit order'.

The second nuclear power programme

Despite the problems, British governments continued to put faith in cost forecasts by nuclear enthusiasts. While the first nuclear programme was still under way, the Labour government (in its 'white heat of technology' phase)[13] decided in 1965 to proceed with a second programme, using another AEA design, the Advanced Gas-cooled Reactor (AGR). This decision has been called 'one of the biggest investment mistakes since the Second World War'.[14] (Fred Lee, Minister of Power, said: 'I am quite sure we have hit the jackpot this time'.)

The AGR, a Magnox offshoot, using enriched instead of natural uranium, was chosen after a CEGB/AEA appraisal suggested a 7 per cent cost advantage over the American Boiling Water Reactor (BWR).[15] Meanwhile the nuclear industry in the USA, where there was some competition, had decided not to proceed with the Magnox reactor, preferring water-cooled reactors to gas-cooled.

---

13 An expression Harold Wilson coined in opposition.

14 Dieter Helm, *Energy, the State and the Market*, Oxford University Press, 2004, p. 90.

15 Boiling Water Reactors (BWRs) and Pressurised Water Reactors (PWRs) are two types of Light Water Reactor (LWR). Heavy Water Reactors (HWRs), in contrast, use 'heavy water' wherein the isotope deuterium partly or wholly replaces hydrogen in the molecules.

(There was 'great difficulty ... finding a site in Britain suitable for the intrinsic hazards of ... a [water] reactor'.)[16]

Duncan Burn, a rare British critic of the decision, noted that the assessors had 'given the benefit of many doubts to the AGR'.[17] The BWR's capital costs and unavailability time both seemed curiously high – with construction costs in Britain apparently 60 per cent more than in the USA. A 600MW AGR unit was being extrapolated from a 30MW prototype, whereas a 200MW BWR had been in commercial operation for years.[18]

Indeed, as with Magnox, costs may have been of minor importance. (For example, there were safety concerns about Light Water Reactors [LWRs].) But there was no agreed method of evaluating reactors and the British appraisal failed to convince others. It later became painfully apparent that the AGR had been far from ready for commercial construction, and no overseas buyer ever placed an order for one. The obvious question was whether it would have paid to import reactors from abroad. At this time the British government was controversially deciding to scrap the TSR-2 bomber in favour of the American F-111, and it might have been awkward to buy American in nuclear power as well. (Perhaps it would have been better to go instead for the British bomber and the American reactor.)

In fact there was serious friction between the CEGB and the AEA in the early 1960s. Sir Christopher Hinton, now CEGB chairman, believed the AEA should not embark on expensive prototype work without taking their main potential user with

16   Gowing, op. cit., vol. 2, p. 264.

17   Burn, op. cit., p. 12.

18   Richard Pryke, *The Nationalised Industries: Policies and Performance since 1968*, Martin Robertson, 1981, p. 27.

them. It was not for the AEA to be the ultimate arbiter of commercial policy. Hinton later criticised splitting reactor design between the CEGB (customers), the consortia (manufacturers) and the AEA (a separate research body). He thought such a three-cornered set-up 'in which argument can go in circles' unlikely to succeed.[19]

At about this time there were also arguments about the relative cost of coal. Lord Robens, chairman of the National Coal Board, believed the AGR programme was being subsidised.[20] He complained that while the costs of coal were known, those of nuclear energy were not, and he criticised the civil servants in the Ministry of Power as being 'birds of passage' who never really got to grips with the details. In the summer of 1962 the Powell committee was set up to look into reactor choice and reconcile different views about the economics of nuclear and conventional power. But no record of its discussions was ever published. *Nature*[21] called such secrecy indefensible. 'Informed comment and discussion are both impossible if the government withholds from publication all the technical considerations on which its decision … is based.' And the *New Scientist*[22] argued that poorer decisions would result from a secret technocracy than from a more open system.

The second nuclear power programme, like the first, suffered from serious cost overruns, construction delays and operating problems. It was soon obvious that there were significant design problems with the first AGR (Dungeness B), but the industry went ahead and ordered four more. The financial risks from building

19   Hinton, *New Scientist*, 28 October 1976, p. 202.

20   Williams, op. cit., p. 158.

21   *Nature*, 202, 27 June 1964, pp. 1247–8.

22   *New Scientist*, 19 March 1964.

nuclear power stations remained extremely high. In 1973 the CEGB concluded[23] that AGRs were about 25 per cent more expensive than LWRs; and Sir Arnold Weinstock, chairman of GEC, said LWRs would have been a better choice.

In a detailed study, Henderson[24] reckoned the *extra* costs of AGRs versus LWRs (*including* interest) was £2,100 million in 1975 prices (**£12,500 million**). He estimated net costs and returns year by year both for the AGR programme and for the alternative, which he took to be an LWR programme.[25] (This seems a convincing assumption, given the UK climate of the late 1960s.) He reckoned an average LWR delay in construction of one and a half years compared with an average five-year AGR delay (making the 'charitable' assumption of no further AGR shocks).

The target had been to build 8,000MW of AGR plant by 1975 in five stations. In 1978 two more AGR stations (Heysham II and Torness) were added with a total output of 2,500MW. But by 1989 only about 7,300MW of AGRs were in commission (see Table 5), a shortfall of nearly 40 per cent for the five English stations. The average output was 1,050MW compared with a target of 1,600MW. There had been industrial relations problems and acute technical difficulties. The last AGR reactors were fully commissioned only in the early 1990s – some fifteen years behind schedule.

---

23 Williams, op. cit., p. 222.

24 P. D. Henderson, 'Two British errors: their probable size and some possible lessons', *Oxford Economic Papers*, 1977, pp. 159–205.

25 '[T]he AGR programme looks much better if one compares it with a conventional [fossil fuel] alternative.' Henderson, op. cit., p. 184.

Table 5 **The second nuclear programme's stations**

Second nuclear programme 10,500MW	Actual net output MW	Consortium
Dungeness B	720	Atomic Power Construction (BNDC)
Hartlepool	840	British Nuclear Design & Construction
Heysham I	840	British Nuclear Design & Construction
Hinkley Point B	1,120	The Nuclear Power Group
Hunterston B*	1,150	The Nuclear Power Group
Heysham II	1,230	British Nuclear Design & Construction
Torness*	1,400	National Nuclear Corporation
Total	7,300	

*SSEB: others for CEGB.

Some of the construction delays verged on the incredible. The AGR power station Dungeness B turned out to be one of the most dismal failures in the history of nuclear power. It was due to be commissioned in 1970 with output of 1,200MW. But the Atomic Power Construction consortium that put in the (disputed) winning tender for the station went out of business within a few years and the project then encountered very serious technical and labour relations problems. It was *22 years* before Dungeness B produced any power at all.[26]

British nuclear power was much more expensive than the alternatives, whether different nuclear reactors or fossil fuel. It did not even enhance security of supply, since most of the AGRs came

---

26   Helm, op. cit., p. 104.

on-stream long after their due dates. As a result other sources of energy – coal, oil or natural gas – had to make up for the missing nuclear output. Luckily consumption grew more slowly than the government had expected, which reduced the scale of the problem.

Towards a third 'programme'

In the 1970s, decisions about nuclear power were entirely in the hands of politicians and the AEA and CEGB. All of them were keen on large investment in nuclear power to safeguard against insecure fossil fuel supplies and price increases; though there continued to be disputes about which type of reactor to go for. The oil 'shocks' of 1973–74 and 1979–80 reinforced these beliefs. But the short time horizon of political decision-makers contrasted with the technology's timescale measured in decades.[27]

By the early 1970s the CEGB, disappointed with AGRs, was ordering mainly oil-fired power stations, rather than either coal-fired or nuclear stations. Arthur Hawkins, then chairman, described it as a 'catastrophe' to allow three different AGR designs for the first four stations. He argued for US Pressurised Water Reactors (PWRs), but the government continued to prefer a British design – 'a needless addiction to indigenous technology'.[28] Sir Alan Cottrell, the government's chief scientist, was worried about safety aspects of the LWR. Both government and industry were reluctant to build more AGRs, but the NII, lacking necessary staff, would take up to two years to give the LWR safety clearance.[29]

---

27 The argument that capital markets are short-termist too is ably countered by Paul Marsh, *Short-Termism on Trial*, Institutional Fund Managers' Association, 1990.

28 Nigel Lawson, *The View from No. 11*, Bantam Press, 1992, pp. 166–7.

29 Pryke, op. cit., p. 44.

So in 1974 the government selected the Steam Generating Heavy Water Reactor (SG-HWR), another AEA design. This risked the same 'scaling-up' mistake as with the AGR earlier, since the only experience of an SG-HWR had been with the 100MW prototype at Winfrith. The SG-HWR was favoured by Sir Francis Tombs, then chairman of the SSEB, but not by Hawkins, the CEGB chairman. He said it was for the government to decide, as between nuclear power and alternatives; but they could not be expected to understand nuclear technology.[30] Tombs made a similar point after later becoming chairman of the Electricity Council. By January 1978, however, it had become clear that the SG-HWR was nowhere near the commercial stage. The government then authorised construction of Heysham II and Torness, which turned out to be the most successful AGRs.

Nuclear cost estimates, little better than guesses, were not decisive in choosing between reactors. Degree of provenness, safety, export potential, economies of scale were all relevant. The Science Committee in 1976 commented: 'It is a sad reflection on … the quality of the expert advice … that, seven years after the last nuclear station was ordered, and after extensive private and public debate, sufficient information is apparently still not available … to proceed with confidence …'[31] David Howell, former Minister of State for Energy, said in 1974: '… the last twenty years in nuclear reactor systems [show] that in government our decision-making procedures have been weak'.

From the start, both the nuclear establishment and the government thought the Fast Breeder Reactor (FBR)[32] would be best for

---

30   Williams, op. cit., p. 245.

31   Ibid., p. 252.

32   Gowing, op. cit., vol.2, p. 270.

the long run. It had no moderator and used uranium much more efficiently[33] than Magnox, AGR or PWR. Britain had experience of it from the experimental breeders at Dounreay. In 1974 British Nuclear Fuels Limited wanted to construct a new thermal oxide fuel reprocessing plant (THORP) at Windscale. It would be large enough to reprocess increased amounts of spent fuel of foreign origin and would cost about £550 million (**£4,000 million**). THORP was essential to retain the FBR option, though it would not pre-empt the decision. A public inquiry eventually agreed to this.

In the late 1970s the industry still argued that nuclear power was cheap. The CEGB asserted: 'Nuclear power continues to be the most economic choice for electricity generation …'[34] And the Electricity Council agreed.[35] The CEGB planned (with government agreement) to order one nuclear power station a year from 1982, giving a programme of 15GW over ten years.[36] But it turned out that *no* more stations, nuclear or otherwise, were needed for the whole of the 1980s. And in the next decade (the 1990s) almost all new capacity was gas.

Rather than continuing with AEA designs, the CEGB now favoured an overseas reactor. In 1981 it applied to build a PWR (Sizewell B), which it claimed would be lower-cost than either an AGR or a coal-fired station. Despite previous experience, there was *still* remarkable optimism about nuclear costs. The Department of Energy reckoned that if fuels were chosen on 'cost grounds

---

33 'It could in principle make possible a 50-fold increase in uranium utilisation. Even more important, it could burn all the waste uranium, mostly U238, left over from the first reactors.' Williams, op. cit., p. 271.

34 CEGB 1978 Corporate Plan.

35 Electricity Council Medium-Term Development Plan 1979–86, para. x.

36 HoC Official Report, 18 December 1979.

alone', commissioning nuclear plants in the first decade of the new century could be in the (wide) range 24 to 83GW.[37] (In the first six years it has in fact been nil.)

After almost four years, the Sizewell public inquiry inspector concluded that Sizewell B 'is likely to be the least cost choice for new generating capacity'. But oil and other fossil fuel prices declined sharply in the mid-1980s – which made the fossil fuel prices used to justify nuclear investment seem on the high side. One casualty was the FBR programme, on which about £4,000 million at 1988 prices (**£7,500 million**) had been spent.[38] A senior AEA executive had described the introduction of the FBR as 'of more economic significance than North Sea oil'.[39] But because commercial fast breeders would not be needed for 30 to 40 years, the government decided to close the Dounreay 250MW Prototype Fast Reactor.

The CEGB applied for consent to build another PWR at Hinkley Point in Somerset, which led to another public inquiry. But by this time privatisation of the electricity supply industry was going through Parliament and the government announced that construction of Sizewell B alone would satisfy its policy for the time being. So a single station was all that remained of Britain's third nuclear power programme.

Privatisation

Governments, rather than market forces, had initiated all Britain's

37 Department of Energy, Evidence for the Sizewell B Inquiry, October 1982, Table 11.
38 C. Robinson, *The Power of the State*, Adam Smith Institute, 1991, p. 15.
39 T. N. Marsham, 'The fast reactor and the plutonium fuel cycle', *Atom*, November 1977, pp. 297–311.

nuclear power stations. By now they produced about 20 per cent of the country's power. In 1989 electricity privatisation exposed them for the first time to the scrutiny of financial markets. The Conservatives' 1987 election manifesto had promised both to privatise the industry and to develop 'abundant low-cost supplies of nuclear electricity'. The second commitment seemed suspect, since privatisation implied leaving producers free to choose which fuels they used.

The privatisation scheme aimed to divide the CEGB's capacity between two big generators. The larger (National Power) would take over existing nuclear power plant and Sizewell B. To ensure contracts for nuclear plant's expensive output, which cost more than fossil fuel plant output, the government established a Non-Fossil Fuel Obligation (NFFO), which would oblige distributors to take a certain proportion of their electricity from non-fossil sources. Low-cost hydroelectric sources were already fully exploited, while there had been little development of other renewable sources of energy; so the NFFO was really just a protective device for nuclear power. Even so, including nuclear power in the flotation was unpopular in the City. There was reluctance to invest in a company with 25 per cent of its capacity in nuclear plant.

At around this time, the Hinkley Point public inquiry brought out some alarming new facts about nuclear costs. A series of leaks suggested that the CEGB's cost estimates were massive underestimates. Rather than just over 2p/kWh, Hinkley's generating costs were likely to be in the range 8–10p/kWh. When the Hinkley inspector asked the CEGB to explain such a huge discrepancy, the answers seemed unconvincing.[40] Not only were estimates

---

40   See Robinson, op. cit., p. 38.

of nuclear power costs extremely dubious, but not being in the public domain they were usually not even open to criticism.

The state-owned industry worried much less about getting proper estimates of nuclear costs than a competitive market would have done. 'In the atomic energy field in Britain … secrecy having begun as a necessity continued as a convenience and eventually became an obsession.'[41] The Select Committee on Energy argued that the CEGB and National Power did not deliberately mislead the government about nuclear costs. Instead '… they appear to have misled themselves until the onset of privatisation injected more rigour into their costings, causing the spectacular change in the perceived costs of PWR electricity …'[42] This may be too generous a verdict. The size of the cost underestimates even in the late 1980s, after 30 years' experience, seems hard to attribute to mere error. It seems more likely that there was at least an element of deliberate deception, which came to light only when the industry leaders had to take personal responsibility for cost and other specific estimates in the prospectus.

Other leaks indicated a huge increase in the total clean-up costs of nuclear plant. Sir Walter (later Lord) Marshall, then CEGB chairman, revealed[43] that the financial provisions for reprocessing Magnox fuel and decommissioning Magnox power stations were to increase from £2.8 billion (**£4,750 million**) to £6.9 billion (**£11,750 million**). This was an *increase* of **£7,000 million**. Again it is hard to accept such an enormous difference as a simple mistake. The highly uncertain future liabilities in terms

41 Williams, op. cit., p. 324.

42 HoC Energy Committee, *The Cost of Nuclear Power*, Fourth report, Session 1989/90, vol. 1, p. xxxiii.

43 Ibid., paras 16–20.

of decommissioning and waste disposal added to the fears of potential investors. Similar figures for the AGRs might amount to at least £5.0 billion (**£8,800 million**),[44] of which the *increase*, pro rata, might be at least £2.8 billion (**£5,000 million**).

In July 1989 the government withdrew the Magnox plants from the sale and four months later it announced that *all* nuclear plants (including the AGRs) would remain state-owned – by Nuclear Electric for stations in England and Wales and by Scottish Nuclear in Scotland. (In December 1995 both became subsidiaries of British Energy, which was floated on the stock exchange in July 1996 with the government retaining 65 per cent of the shares.)

The new Energy Secretary, John (now Lord) Wakeham, said: '… the Non-Fossil [Fuel] Obligation will be set at a level which can be satisfied without the construction of new nuclear stations beyond Sizewell B'. By now all pretence that nuclear energy was cheap had gone by the board. Mr Wakeham said: 'The government has for some time recognised that our nuclear power is more costly than power from fossil-fuelled generating stations. Nevertheless it has an important role to play in providing diversity of supply and in protecting the environment.'[45]

As the government prepared to privatise electricity, capital markets for the first time began to consider the costs and benefits of nuclear investment. Since some of the costs lie many years in the future, nuclear power's 'true' costs are bound to be subject to massive uncertainties. But a market regime provides incentives to understand them rather than just accept the estimates put forward

---

44 Power in Europe, *UK Nuclear Decommissioning: Just a Round Number*, 26 October 1989.

45 9 November 1989.

by government technocrats. This illustrates Hayek's description[46] of competition as a 'discovery procedure' – the best practical way to try to overcome ignorance.

Summary of 'losses'

There are serious problems in measuring the costs of civilian nuclear power, so it is hard to quantify nuclear power station 'losses' in quite the same way as for the other projects. Helm says: 'The scale of the losses will probably never be known. The nuclear industry has been surrounded by secrecy, conveniently buried in the aggregated CEGB accounts. The capital costs have never been separately identified, joint costs were never fully allocated, and, of course, the linkages to the military programme remain state secrets.'[47]

It seems fair to assume that, at the time they made the decisions, the government believed the first (Magnox) and second (AGR) nuclear power programmes would cost about the same as the best alternatives. If so, we can regard at least the following four very large amounts as 'losses':

- Prototype FBR development costs: **£7,500 million**.
- Extra cost of AGRs versus LWRs: **£12,500 million**.[48]
- Unforeseen increase in Magnox decommissioning costs: **£7,000 million**.
- Unforeseen increase in AGR decommissioning costs: **£5,000 million**.

46 F. A. Hayek, 'Competition as a discovery procedure', in *New Studies in Philosophy, Politics, Economics and the History of Ideas*, Routledge & Kegan Paul, London, 1978, pp. 179–190.

47 Helm, op. cit., p. 188.

48 Including interest.

That gives, *as a minimum*, total 'losses' of **£32,000 million**. But the true amounts for some of these items could well be higher. These are not the total costs of providing civilian nuclear power – they are *losses*. This figure does not include the substantial cost of Magnox construction overruns; it almost certainly understates the cost of AGR overruns; and it ignores THORP. It also ignores intangible items on the 'credit' side, such as national prestige.

Conclusion

The principal causes of Britain's disastrous experience with nuclear power were three interacting state monopolies, supported by an interventionist state. These severely distorted the incentives facing managers in the industry.

The nuclear 'establishment' consisted of the AEA, the CEGB (for a long time), parts of the civil service and numerous research scientists. This group held nearly all the information there was and kept it secret as a rule. Since they would benefit from high government spending on nuclear research, they were motivated to underestimate the costs and overestimate the benefits of nuclear power. Because outsiders knew little and had no incentive to find out more, there were no credible competing estimates to challenge the government 'experts'. As a result the nuclear establishment persuaded British governments to keep on investing in nuclear power. Tony Benn said he had 'never known such a well-organised scientific, industrial and technical lobby ... '[49]

The electricity supply industry had a statutory monopoly, so efficiency pressures were largely absent as consumers had little

49   Williams, op. cit., p. 292.

choice. Governments that distrusted market prices as a way to balance supply and demand stifled any competition from other energy sources; and state barriers to entry enabled electricity companies to charge consumers any (undisclosed) excess nuclear costs without fear of being undercut by new entrants.

Finally there were no capital market pressures. There were no private shareholders, so there was no chance of anyone taking over the industry, dismissing the existing top management and changing the business strategy. Since the government provided all its capital, the state-owned electricity supply industry was immune to the market for corporate control. But as privatisation approached, the importance of capital markets became clear: they promptly put an end to government attempts to privatise National Power, including nuclear plant.

The triple monopoly problem was aggravated by ceaseless government interventions in the electricity supply industry: to persuade the CEGB to use British-mined coal, to build British-designed nuclear power stations and to support the British heavy electrical equipment manufacturing industry, as well as to ban it from using natural gas. In such a context, one could hardly expect the industry to be cost-conscious. It was more important (to senior managers) to keep on the right side of politicians and civil servants. Only when the industry was about to be privatised was there more concern about costs.

The total losses of the civil nuclear power programmes in the UK, including the costly prototype FBR, were at least **£32,000 million** – far more than all the other five projects together. The technical decisions were not easy for politicians (with inadequate knowledge) to make, but (with hindsight) it seems clear there were disastrous mistakes. One was panicking about oil supplies after Suez and *tripling* the first nuclear programme. Another was to go for British AGRs rather than American LWRs for the second nuclear programme. Two persistent errors were to overestimate the growth of consumer demand, leading to over-investing in new energy capacity, and to underestimate both supplies of fossil fuels and the costs of nuclear power, leading to over-investing in new *nuclear* capacity.

Acronyms

AEA	Atomic Energy Authority
AGR	Advanced Gas-cooled Reactor
BWR	Boiling Water Reactor (a type of LWR)
CEGB	Central Electricity Generating Board
FBR	Fast Breeder Reactor
GW	Gigawatts (a thousand million watts)
HWR	Heavy Water Reactor
LWR	Light Water Reactor (either BWR or PWR)
MW	Megawatts (a million watts)
NFFO	Non-Fossil Fuel Obligation
NII	Nuclear Installations Inspectorate
PWR	Pressurised Water Reactor (a type of LWR)
SG-HWR	Steam Generating Heavy Water Reactor
SSEB	South of Scotland Electricity Board
THORP	Thermal Oxide Fuel Reprocessing Plant

5 CONCORDE (1956–1976–2003)

Background

In 1954 two crashes of the Comet, the world's first jet airliner, shocked the British aircraft industry and left America supreme in first-generation big jets. The Royal Aircraft Establishment (RAE) at Farnborough, to its dismay, found the immense US military resources threatening its technical prestige in air development. In 1956 Sir George Edwards, head of Vickers, believing that airline passengers would always buy speed, argued that Britain should abandon subsonic planes.

The RAE too urged that the British should now pioneer the world's first *supersonic* commercial airliner and leapfrog the Americans. As a result the Eden government set up a Supersonic Transport Aircraft Committee (STAC) to see whether supersonic transport (SST) was feasible. All the UK aircraft companies and government establishments and the Cranfield College of Aeronautics pooled their knowledge in STAC. The Treasury was not represented.

In 1959 the STAC report[1] proposed that the British aircraft industry should start serious detailed design work on two new supersonic airliners. One was to be long-range, capable of carrying

---

1   Kenneth Owen, *Concorde: Story of a supersonic pioneer*, Science Museum, London, 2001, Appendix 1, pp. 279–84.

150 passengers non-stop 3,500 miles between London and New York at Mach 1.8[2] (1,200 mph); the other a slower medium-range plane carrying 100 passengers up to 1,500 miles at Mach 1.2 (800 mph). Any speed under Mach 2.0 would be able to use aluminium alloys for the structure. Cruising speeds of Mach 2.6 and above were thought possible, using titanium, but without military support they would take too long to develop.

The cost of the long-haul version of the aircraft, including all research and development up to prototype completion, would be £75–95 million. The medium-range version would cost between £50 million and £80 million. The long-range version should aim to come into service in twelve years' time. The STAC report summary[3] talked about 'a commercial venture of high promise': it reckoned that by 1970 'a total demand for between 150 and 500 supersonic aircraft could arise'.[4]

But the government rejected a proposal based on the STAC report. The project's advocates were led by Aubrey Jones, Minister of Supply (the RAE's parent department). In June 1959, as a strong Europhile, he suggested to the French that they work together with the British to develop a supersonic aircraft. The French were keener on the medium-range version up to 2,000 miles, serving intra-European routes, while the British preferred the long-haul version with a transatlantic range of 3,500 miles. Jones later admitted[5] that his department 'had made no attempt at all to estimate the size of the potential market'.

2   A Mach number relates aircraft velocity to the speed of sound: it varies according to the temperature of the atmosphere. Mach 1 is normally 760 mph at sea level.

3   Owen, op. cit., pp. 282–3.

4   Ibid., p. 27.

5   Annabel May, 'Concorde – bird of harmony or political albatross?', *International Organization*, 33(4), Autumn 1979, p. 486.

Duncan Sandys, head of the new Aviation Ministry, also a Europhile, saw it as vital to build a strong British industry to compete with the Americans. Late in 1959, he encouraged the Bristol Aircraft Company to merge with Vickers Armstrong and English Electric Aviation to form the British Aircraft Corporation (BAC). Sir George Edwards became chairman. At that time the British aircraft industry was three times larger than France's. In October 1960, BAC got a contract to look into a 120-passenger aircraft flying at Mach 2.2.[6] A revised design study later led to a twenty-page report, described as 'little more than a sketch'.

After the USA had rebuffed British suggestions of cooperation over an SST, there was strong American pressure to drop the supersonic proposal. Nevertheless, this twenty-page report formed the basis for an agreement between the British and French governments. The French viewed the SST project as a way to develop and grow their aircraft industry. It was an international treaty rather than a business contract. Enoch Powell, a cabinet minister, later said: 'You use politicians if you want a political result, and businessmen if you want a business result.'[7] According to Peter Jay,[8] a former Treasury official, four red herrings were constantly being employed by its advocates: patriotism, the need to keep up with technological progress, unemployment and the importance of not offending France.

At the second meeting to discuss the SST project in November 1962, the cabinet decided to go ahead. The two governments would share equally research and development costs totalling £160 million (**£2,400 million** in 2007 pounds),

6   Concorde's design speed of Mach 2.2 was about 1,430 mph at 60,000 feet.

7   J. Costello and T. Hughes, *The Battle for Concorde*, Compton Press, 1971, p. 156.

8   *The Times*, 10 December 1971.

with no limit, no provision for review – and no cancellation clause. Both the British Treasury and the French Ministry of Finance objected to that omission. But Julian Amery, then Aviation Minister, the most committed Europhile of all, argued that if Britain pulled out the French would go it alone. He was not a member of the cabinet, but he was Prime Minister Harold Macmillan's son-in-law.

There were two major political aspects. Some ministers believed that Britain needed a project of this size to maintain a viable aircraft industry. Since she could not afford it on her own, joint action with either France or America was essential (but if the British could not afford to go it alone, could the French?). In fact Amery insisted on the 'no cancellation' clause for fear that otherwise the *French* might pull out. Further, in late 1962 Britain needed France's support in her bid to enter the Common Market. In the event, however, only six weeks later President de Gaulle vetoed British entry.

It was at de Gaulle's famous January 1963 press conference that the aircraft was first called 'Concorde'. The name was suggested by the eighteen-year-old son of F. G. Clark, the publicity manager at BAC's Filton plant. Until 1967 the English spelt it 'Concord', without an 'e' at the end. Tony Benn, then Minister of Technology, conceded the change, saying that the letter 'e' 'stood for Excellence, England, Europe and Entente'.

Two weeks before the agreement was signed, Lord Brabazon of Tara, a veteran air expert, voiced strong objections in the House of Lords. He said the cost would be three times the cost of a Boeing 707 and the supersonic aircraft would fail to attract extra traffic. Moreover the projected time savings were unreal since they would be greatly reduced by ground access. Worst of all would be problems of noise and sonic boom. He turned out to be correct on all these matters.

The point about time savings has become even more important in recent years, with time-consuming security delays. If you have to get to an airport two hours in advance, and it takes half an hour to reach the airport and another half-hour to get to your destination, then you are adding three hours to your time in the air. So what may look like a three-and-a-half-hour (Concorde) versus a seven-hour journey could easily turn into a six-and-a-half-hour versus a ten-hour journey – reducing the time saving from one half to one third or even less.

Technology

A supersonic transport (SST) faced immense technical challenges. At Mach 2 the fuselage gets extremely hot, while the atmospheric pressure at 60,000 feet is only one tenth of that at sea level. Military aircraft, with pilots in pressure suits, had ventured more than 10 miles high, though usually only for a few minutes at a time. But an SST had to carry at least a hundred airline passengers at supersonic speed in complete comfort and safety for hours at a stretch. Of course, the aircraft also had to take off and land at *subsonic* speeds.

Many trade-offs were needed: for example, extra strength means extra weight and engines efficient at Mach 2 might be too noisy on take-off. Only 6 per cent of Concorde's total take-off weight was payload (see Table 6), compared with a Boeing 747's payload of 20 per cent. That meant an extremely small margin to spare in planning the weight of the structure, engine and fuel: for example, a 1 per cent increase in fuel would reduce payload by eight passengers (out of one hundred). As a result, throughout the project it was essential to do everything possible to reduce the aircraft's weight.

Mr Thornton, Secretary for Aerospace and Shipping at the Department of Trade and Industry (DTI), pointed out: '... you not only had in the Concorde an extremely advanced technological product ... one that was pushing the state of the art in designing the airframe and engine to the limits – but you also had the difficulty of the very small margins that we were working with. [This] combination makes the thing as a whole just about the most speculative kind of project one could imagine'.

Table 6 **Make-up of Concorde's gross weight**

	'000lbs	Tons
Fuel*	200	89
Structure, furnishings and equipment	123	55
Power plant	52	23
	375	167
Payload	25	11
Gross weight	400	178

* Fuel made up half the total weight, owing to the very heavy fuel consumption per mile.

The supersonic art was in a rather primitive state, so there were bound to be many improvements as the work progressed. While these were very welcome, they did take time – and add to the costs. It was not that the project greatly exceeded budgeted spending year by year, but the future work still needing to be done kept expanding.

After a time it became apparent that the original specification simply would not meet requirements, so the plane had to be redesigned. Important early changes increased engine thrust and wing area to ensure regular and safe transatlantic crossings and to meet noise standards. Later major alterations to the fuselage, wings and engine nozzles increased fuel capacity and passenger payload. In 1965 the payload was increased from 90 to 118 passengers, and in 1967 from 118 to 130.[9] All these changes were very expensive, but in effect both governments gave their aircraft industries *carte blanche* on Concorde.

As a result, there were three very different versions of Concorde – the prototype, the pre-production aircraft and the production series (see Table 7).

Table 7 **Details of three different versions of Concorde**

	Prototype	Pre-production	Production
Length (ft)	184	193	204
Fuel ('000lbs)	174	190	206
Take-off weight ('000lbs)	326	367	385

Before it could enter service, Concorde required 5,500 hours of flight testing, about four times as many as for a similar-size subsonic aircraft. Sir James Hamilton, Director-General (Concorde) at the Ministry of Aviation, said: 'I was obsessed with safety. I always had before me the example of the R.101, where under political pressure that vehicle was sent off on its maiden operational flight totally unprepared.'[10]

The problem of noise was not new. Back in 1960 Rolls-Royce engineers had signalled a conflict between the aircraft's need for *performance*, implying a conventional turbojet engine, and the

9   Andrew Wilson, *The Concorde Fiasco*, Penguin, Harmondsworth, 1973, p. 92.
10   Owen, op. cit., p. 62.

need for *quietness*, implying a bypass engine. Rolls suggested designing the engine for 100 Perceived Noise Decibels, the standard for the new generation of subsonics. But BAC's Bristol division proposed using their existing Olympus engine, intended for the TSR-2 bomber, so Concorde used four Olympus 593 engines. When TSR-2 was cancelled, instead of the defence budget bearing a large proportion, all the remaining costs of developing the engine fell upon Concorde.

The aircraft aimed to be no noisier on take-off and landing than current subsonic jets. But 'current' meant 'in 1962' rather than 'when Concorde came into service' (in 1976) – by which time the noise of subsonic aircraft was much lower. From the late 1960s in both Britain and America there were also widespread protests against the sonic boom problems of SSTs. These became critical for long flights over land and resulted in Concorde not being allowed to fly supersonically over Europe.[11] Both these two aspects of noise created a big public relations problem for the aircraft.

In June 1963 President Kennedy announced that the USA too would develop an SST; and the government would bear 75 per cent (later 90 per cent) of the costs. The huge swing-wing Boeing (B2707-200) was to be 318 feet long (about 50 per cent longer than Concorde). Using titanium, it aimed to carry more than three hundred passengers at Mach 2.7 over 3,900 miles at 70,000 feet. But it proved too ambitious. General Maxwell, the SST director, commented wryly: 'We had an aircraft that would go all the way

---

11 For different reasons, the R.101 airship and Concorde both ended up more suitable for flying over oceans than over land. Airships found it difficult coping with gusty air currents over land, while sonic booms made Concorde unwelcome over heavily populated territory.

across the Atlantic empty, but the airlines wouldn't like that; or it could go halfway across with a full load, but the passengers wouldn't like that!'

In 1969 Boeing switched to the version without swing-wings (B2707-300), which would carry 250 passengers over 3,500 miles. But, with growing political pressure, based on costs and noise, this plane too was cancelled two years later. In total the abortive SST programme cost US taxpayers more than $1,000 million (**£4,000 million**). As a result the Anglo-French project, rather than having a three-year lead, ended up with a lead of ten years or more.

Where the Americans failed expensively, the British and French succeeded expensively. It had been hoped that the first prototype would fly in late 1966, with the first Certificate of Airworthiness due at the end of 1969. In the event the first proto-type flew in March 1969, and Concorde finally received its Certif-icates of Airworthiness in late 1975. More than a dozen years of prodigous work had resulted in a marvellous, if belated, technical success.

Organisation

Article 4 of the Anglo-French agreement stated: 'In order to carry out the project, integrated organisations of the airframe and engine firms shall be set up.' This was a demanding requirement, since French and English engineers were very different. French elite technocrats had trained in the academic disciplines of the Ecole Polytechnique, whereas the British had had a long practical apprenticeship on the shop floor.

Harold Macmillan remarked:

> The difference is temperamental and intellectual. It is based
> on a long divergence of two states of mind and methods of
> organisation. The continental tradition likes to reason *a
> priori* from the top downwards, from the general principle
> to the practical application. It is the tradition of St. Thomas
> Aquinas … The Anglo-Saxons like to argue *a posteriori* from
> the bottom upwards, from practical experience. It is the
> tradition of Bacon and Newton.[12]

Moreover they did not use the same language or system of
measurement or currency. Basic differences in national style and
approach persisted throughout the project. The French were more
hierarchical, while the British tended to regard a firm instruction
from above merely as a basis for discussion.[13] Article 4 aimed to
ensure that more than one group looked carefully at everything.
The binational arrangement no doubt delayed decisions, though
once made perhaps the decisions were more likely to be right.

Having equal partners also increased costs, possibly by as much
as one third. Hamilton said: 'The fact that two governments and
four companies had to be satisfied before you made [important
changes] meant that it was … enormously long-winded.' According
to one BAC team member: 'Each quarter we had to submit a pile of
reports over one and a half feet thick.' Brian Trubshawe, the chief
British test pilot, complained it could take nearly two days flying
600 miles from Bristol or Heathrow to Toulouse for a two-hour
meeting. The cost in time, travel and hotel expenses was very high.

---

12 Quoted in Peter Hennessey, *Having It So Good*, Allen Lane, London, 2006, pp. 285–6.
13 Reminiscent of the Duke of Wellington's alleged comment on his first cabinet meeting
    as prime minister: 'An extraordinary affair. I gave them their orders and they wanted
    to stay and discuss them.'

As a result of the agreement there was no one person in charge. Having one person in charge *might* have engendered more 'drive' – but it would have been riskier. In fact there were a number of committees. The Concorde Directing Committee, comprising senior civil servants, controlled the funds and supervised the project, while the Concorde Management Board managed the technical details. In both cases there was a British or French chairman, who would alternate every two years. In practice the chairmen were by no means supreme. They had no casting vote because there were no votes, only consensus.

Under the Management Board were the Aircraft Committee and the Engine Committee. They each comprised a managing director and deputy, a technical director and deputy, a production director and deputy, and two joint sales directors; with the Aircraft Committee also having a director from BAC and Sud-Aviation. The main Concorde contractors for the airframe were BAC (40 per cent) and Sud-Aviation (60 per cent) and for the engines Rolls-Royce (60 per cent) and Snecma (40 per cent).

Under the terms of the treaty both sides were to get an equal share of the work. Politics imposed a need to divide the workload and choose which factories to use. There had to be three options for everything: then the two ministries would decide which supplier would get the contract. As a result the final choice of suppliers did not always correspond with the design team's wishes.

Moreover, the use of American and other equipment complicated the process. For example, the generators began as a UK design, then changed to a French one, then to a US design with some UK involvement, then to a UK design, and finally to a combined alternator/constant-speed drive of US design and

UK manufacture. For the hydraulic pumps, the first design was British, the second was an unsuccessful French attempt to scale up an existing American pump, and the third was a US design made in Germany.

A complex system of manufacture evolved with plants throughout the two countries making parts for the two assembly lines. Duplicating assembly lines (at Filton, north of Bristol, and Toulouse in southern France) was itself expensive in forgoing learning-curve effects. UK test flights took place at Fairford, north of Swindon – an hour by road from Filton. A 1970 survey showed that over seven hundred British companies were supplying Concorde and many gained expertise from working on the aircraft's advanced technology.

Costs

The House of Commons Estimates Committee[14] concluded that the research and development cost estimates of £160 million (**£2,400 million**) were speculative; the Treasury expected costs to be much higher;[15] and the British government had 'entered into a binding commitment with the French government for the development of this project with an imprecise knowledge of the probable cost'. The assumption that the aircraft might be able to recover its costs on sales of 150 to 200 aircraft was equally uncertain – since there was no assurance that sales of that order would be achieved.

In mid-1964 the Chief Secretary to the Treasury told the cabinet that even on present estimates: 'the project would cost nearly as much as two Channel Tunnels'. The Committee of

14   HoC Estimates Committee, Seventh Report, Session 1963/64.
15   The Treasury was reported to be 'multiplying the estimated costs by pi' (i.e. by 3.14)!

Public Accounts[16] in 1965 doubted 'the value of estimates which are so conjectural as to be almost worthless as an indication of the ultimate cost'. There was no guarantee that the plane would even be able to fly from London to New York.

In late 1964 Roy Jenkins, Minister of Aviation, had to tell the French government that the British were cancelling the Concorde project (on cost grounds). '[They] reacted more in sorrow than anger … [They] always kept in hand … the threat of suing us for damages in The Hague Court of International Justice. This was their trump card … the firm advice of our Law Officers … was that … we would lose and might well have damages of … £200m [**£3,000 million**] awarded against us.'[17]

A few months later the new Labour government reversed its 'decision' to cancel the Concorde. A third formal French note had recently arrived, which 'sounded as firm as could be'. Jenkins says: 'I subsequently received strong … hints that this third note was the last French throw, and that, had we then persisted, they would have accepted that the project was dead, with a bad grace but without going to The Hague Court. … [H]ad we approached the French confidentially a quiet funeral could almost certainly have been arranged.'[18]

Britain wanted to abandon the Concorde project on at least four occasions after 1962,[19] often partly as a result of US pressure. At no stage, however, did a Chancellor of the Exchequer even threaten to resign over the issue: 'the impact of the Concorde spending programme was no doubt too remote and too

---

16   Peter Hall, *Great Planning Disasters*, Penguin, Harmondsworth, 1980, p. 95.

17   Roy Jenkins, *A Life at the Centre*, Macmillan, Basingstoke, 1991, p. 165.

18   Ibid., p. 166.

19   Late 1964, autumn 1967, autumn 1970 and spring 1974.

uncertain'.[20] The French were likewise inclined (though less publicly) at least thrice,[21] but not at the same times as the British. Sustained American pressure to cancel Concorde may actually have hardened the French resolve to persevere.

From this point, the government reviewed the Concorde project every six months. Tony Benn, MP for South-East Bristol, became Minister of Technology in 1967 and took charge of the British side of the project. There is no evidence that the closeness of his South-East Bristol constituency to the Filton assembly line influenced Benn's decisions, as was sometimes suggested. He said Concorde survived '… on the most elaborate calculations of money spent, investment to come, likely returns [and] likely sales'. Even so, 'it was a cost-plus contract with no performance benchmarks or timetable'.[22]

Until 1968 the contracts were on a cost-plus basis. After that there was a complex scheme whereby as costs rose a supplier's profit fell. But if a company could persuade the department to accept extra spending to increase performance, then profits would again increase. So the manufacturers had a positive incentive to suggest changes that would increase their profits further. A 1973 House of Commons committee concluded: '… throughout the Concorde project the contractual arrangements have had definite defects: in particular they have lacked adequate incentives to economy and efficiency and have placed the contractors at no risk'.

There were regular increases in the cost estimates. By June

20 Jock Bruce-Gardyne and Nigel Lawson, *The Power Game: An Examination of Decision-making in Government*, Macmillan, Basingstoke, 1976, p. 161.

21 Early 1965, 1966, mid-1974.

22 Michael Heseltine, *My Life in the Jungle*, Coronet, London, 2000, p. 137.

1973, they had risen[23] from £160 million (**£2,400 million**) to £1,065 million (**£7,800 million**). Owing to very rapid inflation between 1963 and 1973, what looked like an increase of nearly 600 per cent in money terms – and was often quoted as such – was an increase of 'only' just over 200 per cent in 'real' terms of constant purchasing power. About one third of the 'real' increase was due to revision of estimates and about two-thirds to 'additional development tasks'.

But Hamilton said: 'Financial discipline was extraordinarily difficult … It was too big a project in comparison with the total financial resources of the companies involved for us to be able to apply a great contract penalty … The only lever [was] that of cancelling the whole project.' In the early 1970s the Central Policy Review Staff called Concorde 'a commercial disaster', but concluded that, for political reasons, the project must continue.

In March 1974, Tony Benn, Secretary of State for Industry, revealed cost figures for Concorde which until then had remained secret.[24] Research and development costs of £1,070 million (**£8,000 million**) would not be recovered. In addition there would be a production loss of £200 million (**£1,600 million**) on the fleet of sixteen under construction. It would have made no sense to produce fewer than sixteen production Concordes, even though in the event five of them remained unsold. Any temptation to *expand* production in the hope of more future sales, which could have meant further production losses, was resisted. (Apparently

23   Hall, op. cit., p. 95.
24   Elliot J. Feldman, *Concorde and Dissent: Explaining high technology failures in Britain and France*, Cambridge University Press, 1985, pp. 97, 127, 139, says the project was given military priority owing to the technology's potential application: in both Britain and France 'it formally came under military supervision', which guaranteed the secrecy a strictly commercial project could not justify.

in June the French prime minister, Jacques Chirac, told Harold Wilson that he wanted to build 200 Concordes.[25])

Were these huge costs offset by external factors and intangible benefits? Henderson[26] thought there were five items for which one could guess a money value: two positive (technical achievement/prestige and spin-off), two negative (engine noise and overflying rights), and balance of payments effects. The net amounts for the two positive and two negative items, ranging between £10 million and £17 million (in 1975 prices), virtually cancelled each other out. The final item he put at minus £28 million. He concluded that the net total for all items together was so small as to be 'hardly worth bothering about'.

Moreover British Airways (BA) expected to lose money operating Concorde, which the British taxpayer would have to subsidise. The loss would be up to £25 million (**£200 million**) a year: £16 million on Concorde itself and £9 million on forgone business from first-class and business-class travel on subsonic aircraft. British Airways arranged to order Concorde on the understanding that if it worsened the airline's operating surplus there would be a case for government review. Michael Heseltine, the Minister for Aerospace, agreed. In 1979 the £160 million of 'public dividend capital' that BA had used to buy Concordes was written off.

Sales

A 1970 study by the (US) Federal Aviation Agency[27] had suggested

25 Terry Gourvish, *The Official History of Britain and the Channel Tunnel*, Routledge, London, 2006, p. 139 and note 34 on p. 435.

26 Henderson, op. cit., pp. 173–80.

27 Owen, op. cit., p. 235.

a potential total world demand for 500 to 800 SST planes by 1990. Even allowing for an American SST, which then seemed likely, the British reckoned Concorde could capture half of this total. (After the summer of 1963 it was clear that no airline wanted the French medium-range version.)

Sir Archibald Russell, leader of the BAC design team, said: '… any sensible plan to proceed should be on the basis of a strong possibility that the development costs incurred will be recovered by the sales of aircraft'.[28] But he pointed out: 'While the estimation of development expenditure is more an art than a science, it is still vastly more accurate than the prediction of the number of aircraft that will eventually be sold.' However impressive the technical achievement in producing the aircraft, the Concorde project was clearly open to criticism in both these areas. It was called 'the only airplane project ever launched without some preliminary understanding with the airlines of what their requirements were and what the market for it might be'.[29]

By 1967, in return for a small deposit, 74 options on Concorde were outstanding – eight each for BOAC, Air France and Pan American; six each for American Airlines, Eastern Airlines, TWA and United Airlines; and 26 in total for other carriers. As late as 1968 there was no firm estimate of sales. In that year a BAC report suggested that even with a ban on supersonic flying over land, *minimum* sales should total 200 to 250. The joint committee that oversaw the project accepted that figure, which was still being used four years later.

Yet two important changes occurred during those years. The first was the Boeing 747, announced in 1965, which came into

28   Ibid., pp. 49–50.
29   G. Knight, *Concorde: The Inside Story*, Weidenfeld & Nicolson, London, 1976.

service in 1970 as the successor to the 707 – together with parallel US planes such as the Douglas DC-10 and the Lockheed Tristar. (The Treasury had predicted this years before.) The Boeing 747 could carry three times as many people as Concorde. It brought about a rapid reduction in cost per seat-mile on long-haul trips. With the advent of wide-bodied aircraft, the pattern of air traffic began to change; economy and price became critical rather than speed.

At the same time, airline profits began to drop. In the four years to 1966, PanAm averaged annual profits of $52 million; in the four years to 1970, average annual *losses* were $38 million. In January 1970 it cancelled one of its options on Concorde. By late 1972, *before* the first oil shock, most other airlines had cancelled their options too. In January 1973 PanAm and TWA cancelled all their options. PanAm said: '[Concorde] has significantly less range, less payload and higher operating costs than … current and prospective wide-bodied jets, [so] it will require substantially higher fares.'

BAC was left with the argument that if British Airways and Air France bought Concorde, then other airlines would have to buy it too. But none of them did. Concorde offered the advantage of speed plus standard of comfort; but its running costs were very high and noise was a serious problem. By 1978 only sixteen Concordes had been built, and nine sold, all to the captive state airlines of Britain and France. No independent airline chose to buy Concorde, despite a great deal of effort to sell the five aircraft in the shop window. The total cost of research and production to the two countries was about **£9,600 million** – yet in the end they found not a single willing customer.

Operations

Concorde's economics, by normal airline standards, were dreadful. Fares were 20 per cent higher than first-class. Maintenance costs were ten times higher than those of a subsonic aircraft and accounted for more than 40 per cent of the operating costs. The supersonic plane also took up more than its share of BA management time.

In July 1972 BA purchased five Concordes with spares for a total of £115 million (**£850 million**) (**£100 million** per aircraft plus a total of **£350 million** for spares, equipment, hangars, training costs, etc.). The next year the sharp increase in the price of fuel following the Yom Kippur war made the aircraft even more expensive to operate. In 1974 BA reckoned its cost per seat-mile to be more than three times as much as that of a Boeing 747.

But Concorde *was* fast. In June 1974 a French Concorde completed the Paris–Boston–Paris *return* flight in less time than a Boeing 747 took to get from Paris to Boston. The fastest time from London to New York was just under three hours. Concorde was intended for transatlantic flights of about 3,500 miles. She was less suitable for longer hauls, on which the need for refuelling stops tended to nullify her speed advantage. Thus the Boeing 747SP, with a non-stop range of more than 10,000 miles, could fly from London to Sydney faster than Concorde.[30]

Commercial service started in January 1976, with the British Concorde flying from London to Bahrain, and the French Concorde from Paris to Rio de Janeiro. Flights to Washington started in May that year, and to New York eighteen months later. (This was after delays due to serious objections, resolved in

30   Feldman, op. cit., p. 108.

Concorde's favour only by the US courts.) Flights to Washington ended in 1994, since nearly everyone wanted to go to New York. A spare Concorde was standing by at Heathrow every day.

After some years the British government said it would cease funding support costs for Concorde, and asked whether BA wished to take these on. (If not – as the government had expected – it would have meant grounding the aircraft, at least in the UK.) After much haggling, in 1982 BA agreed to pay £16.5 million (**£40 million**) for spares, etc.

In its first ten years, Concorde made 15,000 flights, flying more than 50,000 hours and carrying almost 1 million passengers. Each Concorde averaged 2.33 flying hours per day, compared with 13.66 hours for BA's Boeing 747s. Over the next fifteen years it continued at a slightly more intense level.

In July 2000, a charter Concorde carrying German passengers from Paris to New York crashed soon after take-off. All 100 passengers and nine crew on board were killed, plus four people on the ground. The aircraft ran over a strip of metal from a DC-10 that had just taken off: this cut a tyre and led to the rupture of a fuel tank which caused a serious fire and severe problems in two engines. Air France at once grounded its fleet, and BA did so three weeks later after the suspension of Concorde's Certificate of Airworthiness.

Eighteen months later fare-paying services resumed. But there were a number of operational problems and not long afterwards it was suddenly announced that Concorde's last flight would take place in October 2003 – this although the aircraft was cleared to fly until 2009 (which could have been extended to 2015). After more than 25 years, each Concorde had completed about the same number of flights as a four-year-old Boeing 737.

Conclusion

The Concorde was a tremendous engineering triumph – though the whole project cost about a hundred times as much in real terms as the entire R.101 airship programme. (People have even compared it with the architectural marvels of the world: the Pyramids, the Gothic cathedrals and the Taj Mahal.)

For its promoters, the British and French governments, and for their taxpayers, it was a commercial disaster: after a massive underestimate of construction time and cost, Concorde lost in total about **£9,600 million**. But those who worked on this magnificent aircraft must surely be proud of having done so.

There were two key political errors: a mistaken assumption that working with France on the Concorde project was part of the price for securing entry to the European Common Market, and a propensity to pursue national prestige at almost any cost.

A serious technical oversight was failure to recognise sufficiently the environmental problems both from take-off and landing noise and from sonic booms.

Probably more important was the commercial misconception that speed was the key criterion for an airliner's success, over-optimism in predicting sales and insufficient regard to customer requirements. Indeed, one could argue that there was a reckless failure even to *care* whether or not there was a market.

Acronyms

BAC	British Aircraft Corporation
RAE	Royal Aircraft Establishment
SST	Supersonic transport
STAC	Supersonic Transport Aircraft Committee

6 THE CHANNEL TUNNEL (1985–1994–2007)

England has had no physical link to the continent of Europe for more than eight thousand years. Until now. Proposals to build a tunnel or a bridge between England and France were first made 200 years ago, by Napoleon among others. (He said, 'The Channel is a mere ditch.') But at the end of the nineteenth century and the beginning of the twentieth, British military objections proved persuasive, though Gladstone pointed out that since 1066 England had invaded France much more often than France had invaded England! In 1924 a committee with four former prime ministers rejected a proposal for a twin-bore tunnel costing £29 million (**£1,200 million** in 2007 pounds), believing that security drawbacks outweighed commercial benefits. Many people also felt an emotional – but very real – attachment to Britain's island status.

The first post-war Tunnel project

After World War II military objections faded. But in both countries the cost of building a cross-Channel rail link seemed too high. In 1957 the renamed Suez Canal Company formed a Channel Tunnel Study Group with French and British tunnel companies holding rights in the project from earlier ventures. With American finance, they undertook technical and commercial studies, and there were long debates as to the rival merits of a tunnel or a bridge.

In 1961, when the UK first applied to join the Common Market, the prospect of a Channel Tunnel was a minor element in the talks. In February 1964 the British and French governments agreed that a bored rail tunnel under the Channel could be a good investment. A basic principle,[1] in spirit if not (as with Concorde) in letter, was *moitié-moitié* (half and half); though in practice this had its problems. For example, digging on the French side would be more difficult, hence more expensive, while rail improvements in south-east England would cost more than in northern France.

Labour's National Plan[2] put the cost of a Channel Tunnel at £170 million (**£2,500 million**). In July 1966 an agreement 'in principle' was signed for the private sector to build and finance a tunnel. Government-guaranteed loans would cover most of the cost. On the whole the British government seemed keener on the project than the French (though the French traffic forecasts were higher); while SNCF,[3] the French railways, supported it more than British Rail (BR), which also had interests in car ferries, hovercraft and container ships. But for various reasons, there was little further progress before a Conservative government returned in June 1970.

In November 1972 the two governments, the two state-owned railways and the British and French tunnel companies signed contracts, which later resulted in a Treaty. By then the Tunnel's projected cost had risen to £468 million (**£4,100 million**). Increased oil prices at that time were helpful to Tunnel traffic

---

1   Peter Morris and George Hough, *The Anatomy of Major Projects*, Wiley, 1987, p. 25.

2   *The National Plan*, HMSO, London, Cmnd. 2764, September 1965, p. 131, para. 28.

3   Société Nationale des Chemins de Fer Français.

forecasts, given their effect on the airlines; though it was unclear how they might affect future economic growth.

In addition, the Treaty *required* a high-quality rail link from the Tunnel to London. It would cost a further £120 million (**£1,100 million**), but it was a vital part of the project, in order to compete with the airlines. A high-speed link would reduce the journey time between London and Paris by about an hour, to two and a half hours. But there was no agreement about its route. BR wanted a terminal at White City, where it owned land; the Greater London Council preferred Surrey Docks, attracted by the potential improvement of London's Docklands; while the Department of the Environment favoured Victoria for its central London location.

By May 1974 the cost of the rail link had risen to £375 million[4] (**£2,800 million**). This dramatic increase was due to several things: additional facilities, design and development, environmental factors and underestimates. The new cost seemed excessive, so six months later the Wilson government dropped the high-speed rail link, while looking again at a cheaper and slower alternative.

By January 1975 a few hundred yards of tunnel had been bored on each side of the Channel. At that point, the Labour government abandoned the Tunnel project itself too, mainly for cost reasons. (The actual cost of construction, both for the Tunnel and for the high-speed rail link, would probably have greatly exceeded the latest estimates.) The abandonment triggered generous compensation payments to the equity investors in the British and French tunnel companies, totalling about **£250 million**.

Terry Gourvish states flatly that 'two fundamental misjudge-

---

4   Terry Gourvish, *The Official History of Britain and the Channel Tunnel*, Routledge, London, 2006, p. 140.

ments were made':[5] John Peyton, the transport minister, tying in the rail link so closely with the Channel Tunnel, and BR insisting on a high-speed (and therefore high-cost) rail link option. But both may have seemed essential to generate high enough traffic forecasts to make the project look worthwhile. The high-speed rail link to London is an *essential* part of the Channel Tunnel project.[6] (Hence the subsequent Channel Tunnel was a 'government' project even though government money mainly financed only the high-speed rail link, not the Tunnel itself.)

In the twelve years 1964–75 the party in power in the UK changed three times and there were six different ministers of transport. Given BR's lukewarm attitude towards the Tunnel, so much chopping and changing can hardly have helped. But the project itself was not party-political. Douglas-Home's Conservative government started it, Wilson's (first) Labour government signed an agreement 'in principle', and Heath's Conservative government signed legal contracts and the Treaty. Finally Wilson's (second) Labour government cancelled first the high-quality rail link to London, then the Tunnel itself.

Background to the second Tunnel project

In the early 1980s Mrs Thatcher expressed interest in a fixed link between England and France, which she had supported as a member of the Heath government. The French were keen, in order to regenerate the Nord-Pas de Calais region. At first she and François Mitterrand, the French President, preferred a road to a rail link (as had Heath): he wanted a bridge while she favoured a

---

5   Ibid., p. 168.
6   *The Economist*, 24 March 1973, p. 80, supports this view.

drive-through tunnel. But she ruled out any government finance, and doubted whether a private enterprise rail tunnel would pay.

In April 1985 the two governments invited promoters to submit bids to finance, construct and operate a fixed cross-Channel link, without government funds or guarantees. In February 1986 they signed a Channel Tunnel Treaty to supervise all matters relating to constructing and operating the link. The two parliaments ratified it the next year. By now there had been another six UK ministers of transport, though Andrew Lyall, a Tunnel supporter, had been head of the Department of Transport's International Division for five years.

Many people opposed the Tunnel in England (though fewer in France), mostly on environmental grounds. Ferry companies complained about the possible loss of 6,000 jobs and also played on the public's dread of a fire in a Channel Tunnel. But the *Herald of Free Enterprise* disaster badly undermined the boast that ferries were safe: a roll-on/roll-off passenger and freight ferry capsized and sank off the coast of Zeebrugge on 6 March 1987, with the loss of 193 lives.

From the nine fixed-link bids, four contenders formed the shortlist:

- Eurobridge: twelve-lane suspension road bridge, with optional rail link
- Channel Expressway: twin 11.3-metre-bore road tunnel, separate rail tunnel
- EuroRoute: part-bridge, part-tunnel road and rail link
- CTG-FM: twin 7.3-metre-bore rail tunnel for rail and shuttle traffic.

The choice was about the proposals' financial and technical viability, not the management competence of would-be owner-operators. Three of the promoters were partnerships between construction companies and banks: contractors wanted to *build* the Tunnel, banks wanted to *lend* to it, but neither wanted to own and operate the project. The remaining bidder, Channel Expressway, was headed by James Sherwood, CEO of Sea Containers, which owned Sealink ferries. The Treasury opposed all four schemes.

Cost and technical risk ruled out Eurobridge. Of the remaining three bids, the British government preferred Channel Expressway, but there were ventilation problems; and the French government wanted EuroRoute, but there were environmental problems and it would cost the most.

CTG-FM (which became Eurotunnel) was a partnership between the Channel Tunnel Group Limited of the UK and France Manche SA, with no drive-through road option. It was both governments' low-cost, low-risk second choice, and would be the easiest to finance. It could provide a fast, frequent, reliable and comfortable link between the UK and mainland Europe for freight, cars and passengers. The promoters also undertook to submit proposals later for a drive-through road link by 2000,[7] if demand and technology permitted, though this offer seems afterwards to have been silently dropped. Early in 1987 Eurotunnel said it was already working on plans for a drive-through second tunnel,[8] being so certain that demand would quickly overwhelm the first!

So in the end, early in 1986, Eurotunnel was the winner of the

7   Gourvish, op. cit., pp. 274, 276.
8   Drew Fetherston, *The Chunnel*, Times Books, London, 1997, p. 192.

concession, at a projected total construction cost of £2,500 million (**£5,200 million**). The company would design and construct the rail and service tunnels under the Channel together with the passenger and freight terminals at either end. In addition it would provide the special shuttles, the track itself, the advanced signalling and control systems and a wide spectrum of other services.[9] There were two key requirements: to complete construction within ten years, and to maintain and keep open the Tunnel throughout. Failure in either could result in loss of the concession.

The concession gave the right to build and operate the system for 55 years from 1987 (about 49 years from the expected 1993 opening date). Eurotunnel would be free to determine its own commercial policy, including tariffs. There could be no competing fixed link without Eurotunnel's approval before the end of 2020. At the end of the concession, the system would become the property of the British and French governments.

Organisation

There were four main 'producer' stakeholders: Eurotunnel, its shareholders, the banks and the constructors. Eurotunnel, the promoter, would operate the Tunnel once it was open. Shareholders invested £1,023 million equity capital in Eurotunnel up front, in three instalments. The banks lent the company £5,000 million (to begin with): there were five arranging banks, four agent banks and over two hundred underwriting banks. The contractor was TML (TransManche-Link), a joint venture between Translink of the UK and Transmanche Construction of France. (Each of

---

9   Graham Anderson and Ben Roskrow, *The Channel Tunnel Story*, Chapman and Hall, 1994, p. 49.

these was itself a joint venture between five leading construction companies.) Their task was to design and construct the Tunnel.

Time was critical. The constructors reckoned they needed eight years to design and build the Tunnel; but the banks thought the project viable only if it could be done in seven.[10] This was extremely tight. The contract called for construction of the Tunnel within seven years, and contained penalties for time overruns. TML was liable to pay damages of £0.33 million for every day the project overran the deadline (£0.5 million per day beyond six months late).

Interest on borrowed money would cost about £1 million a day, and lost revenue perhaps a further £1 million a day. So time really was money for Eurotunnel, and constructors' damages for delay by no means covered it. Indeed, a one-year delay could cost Eurotunnel around £500 million net,[11] half the initial equity capital.

When Eurotunnel won the concession early in 1986, the bankers formed themselves into the 'agent banks', while the constructors formed TML. So Eurotunnel itself was left as a weak organisation. To begin with the staff consisted mainly of secondees, who then had to negotiate the construction contract with the firms from which they had come. Following the Equity Two issue in October 1986, the Bank of England was very keen to strengthen Eurotunnel's top management. In February 1987, Alastair Morton, by no means the first choice, succeeded Lord Pennock as British co-chairman.

---

10   Fetherston, op. cit., p. 111.
11   Say interest of £350 million a year plus lost revenue of £300 million a year, less damages of £150 million (£60 million at £0.33 million per day for 180 days + £90 million at £0.5 million per day for 180 days).

The construction contract, signed in August 1986, set out the arrangement between Eurotunnel and TML. Total construction costs were then estimated at **£5,000 million**.

Target works (tunnels, underground structures and related equipment) (£1,100 million [**£2,300 million**]) were to be paid for on a cost plus 12.36 per cent fee basis. TML would get 50 per cent of any savings, compared with target costs, but would pay 30 per cent of any excess.

Lump sum works (£1,020 million [**£2,200 million**]) were terminal buildings, infrastructure and roads, fixed equipment, and mechanical and electrical elements of the system, such as signalling. They would be paid for on a lump-sum basis (adjusted for inflation), with TML getting any savings in full but *paying in full for any cost overspend*.

Procurement items (£233 million [**£500 million**]) (rolling stock, mainly locomotives and shuttle trains) would be subcontracted. TML would receive its direct costs of supervision, plus an 11.5 per cent fee on the items' value. There would be two types of trains: high-speed through trains; and specially designed shuttle trains carrying road vehicles and their passengers between the two terminals.

There were concerns that the construction contract would give TML the wrong incentives in three respects: to let costs increase, to stint on quality, and to ignore the tight construction timetable that was critical to Eurotunnel's success. The banks wanted fixed prices, to reduce their risk, but with the design not yet complete, there were bound to be changes in the scope of the work. In the event, lack of mutual trust between Eurotunnel, the constructors and the banks made things very difficult.

Eurotunnel appointed two independent project managers

to monitor the tunnel's design, development and construction. These '*maîtres d'oeuvres*' were Atkins and the Société d'Etudes Techniques et Economiques, but there were worries that they were too close to the constructors. So a third, American, firm, Louis Berger Associates, was appointed as a consultant to the technical agent banks.

The British and French governments set up an Inter-Governmental Commission (IGC) to supervise all matters concerning the construction and operation of the fixed link, and a Safety Authority to advise and assist the IGC. These two bodies had no need to concern themselves with costs, so, like many regulators, they turned out to be extremely risk-averse.

These arrangements led to big problems with divided powers. Eurotunnel had two co-chairmen; TML had two directors-general; a small number of 'agent' banks spoke for 200 lending banks; and the IGC and Safety Authority had power too. Moreover, the main users, BR and SNCF, were also interested parties. With the governments mostly standing aside, there was no single person driving the project forward.

Eurotunnel finance

The promoters of this privately financed project had to meet total costs (in 1987 prices) of £4,850 million, plus contingencies. This would cover construction, corporate and other costs, inflation and net financing costs. Eurotunnel planned to raise about £1,000 million of equity and £5,000 million of loans (giving a starting debt/equity ratio of 500 per cent).

The equity was to be raised in three stages. Equity One, in September 1986, provided no new cash: founding shareholders merely converted earlier loans into £47 million of equity. Equity Two, in October 1986 (three months late), aimed to place shares with financial institutions to raise £206 million. This would enable TransManche-Link to pay its early bills, including those for tunnel-boring machines (TBMs). (It also had the effect of turning the various construction companies into minority shareholders.) But the ferry companies, trying to cast doubt on the project, were publicly *opposing* the issue (which is almost unheard of).

Many institutions were reluctant to subscribe for Equity Two, until the Bank of England agreed to strengthen the Eurotunnel board. Even so, there was a shortfall of about £20 million on the British side, which the leading banks had to take on. *The Economist* acutely remarked: 'If travellers prove half as reluctant to use it as institutional investors have been to invest in it, the Channel Tunnel is in deep trouble.'[12] And it was a worrying omen for Equity Three, aiming to raise £770 million (the balance of the £1,023 million) from the public a year later.

Alastair Morton and André Benard, Eurotunnel's co-chairmen, organised the £5,000 million loans in August 1987 from 50 banks (syndicated globally); £1,000 million came from the European Investment Bank (EIB), and another £1,000 million was on a stand-by basis. It was the largest and longest project financing deal ever arranged, lasting up to eighteen years, and it was a huge struggle – especially as there was very little US involvement. At this time the Tunnel project was expected to cost around £5,000 million, including interest, of which £3,000 million (**£6,000 million**) was for construction. The interest rate would be about 1 per cent a year higher during the construction period.

12   *The Economist*, 1 November 1986, p. 66.

The credit agreement was signed early in November 1987; though Eurotunnel could draw no money until after the public Equity Three flotation of 220 million shares at £3.50 per share to raise £770 million. This had been delayed from July to mid-November 1987 (requiring a short-term loan of £70 million), and was not helped by the October stock market crash. Three business factors were critical to Eurotunnel's operating success: construction overruns, the volume of traffic, and the level of tariffs. The projected profits, and the equity prospects, were highly sensitive to changes in any of the three. Lex, in the *Financial Times*, had earlier noted that investors had to 'discount quite awesome financial, geological and traffic risks'.[13]

Of the 101 million Equity Three shares on offer to British investors, 42 million had already been allocated to certain institutional investors and their clients; which left 59 million for the general public. Of these 39 million were subscribed for, leaving 20 million shares (one third of the British shares available) with the underwriters. The public equity issue was heavily promoted and expenses totalled £68 million (nearly 10 per cent of the gross proceeds). After one day the shares were quoted at £2.50, £1.00 down on the offer price.

The shares in Eurotunnel reached a peak of £11.72 in early June 1989, but after various problems during that summer, the price had halved by October. As costs rose during construction, Eurotunnel (now technically in default on its loan agreement) had to raise more money. In November 1990 (after much argument) a further £1,800 million loan was agreed, plus £300 million from the EIB, together with an extra £566 million equity. The banks were

---

13   *Financial Times*, 23 June 1986.

unhappy, but it was not feasible to replace Eurotunnel as operator or TML as constructor. The 'agent banks' covered a loan 'shortfall' of £250 million. Nearly all the equity shares were subscribed for. In the prospectus for the 1990 equity issue, construction costs alone were now put at £4,208 million (at 1985 prices [**£9,000 million**]).

Thus most of Eurotunnel's fund-raising turned out to be a close shave: Equity Two and Three, and the huge loans arranged in August 1987 and in November 1990. This was where Morton, with his finance background and his negotiating drive, was indispensable.

In May 1994 Eurotunnel announced another equity issue, to raise a further £816 million, along with increased senior debt of £693 million. That brought the total money raised by the time the Tunnel opened to about £2,400 million (**£4,000 million**) of equity and £7,800 million (**£12,500 million**) of debt. That was to cover corporate costs and interest, as well as the costs of construction.

The very high financial gearing left the equity position vulnerable when both costs and construction time overran. And the final straw was customer demand turning out to be less than half the level forecast. Then imposing very high financial risk on fairly high business risk proved disastrous for Eurotunnel's equity shareholders (and, indeed, for many of the lenders).

Construction

The Eurotunnel System was to comprise:

- Twin rail tunnels and a service tunnel under the Channel.
- Two terminals, at Cheriton, near Folkestone, and Coquelles, near Calais.

- Shuttles to carry passenger and freight vehicles between the terminals.
- Inland clearance terminals for freight at Ashford and at the French terminal.
- Connections to nearby railways and roads.

In December 1987 the first tunnel-boring machine started on the English side and two months later on the French side. In total eleven huge TBMs were used. In fact there were twelve tunnels: a service tunnel and two running tunnels on both the English and French sides, both landward and seaward. Each of the two running tunnels and the service tunnel took between two and three years to complete. In total there was about one hundred miles of tunnel. At the peak of tunnelling, in June 1991, TML was employing over eight thousand workers in England and nearly six thousand in France.

Tunnelling had been difficult (during construction there were ten deaths): while the technology of bored tunnels was well understood, there were some unexpected geological problems, especially on the English side. On 30 October 1990 an English probe reached the French service tunnel works and joined the two countries. The main 7.6-metre twin bores were finished in June 1991, six weeks ahead of schedule. Even more challenging was the task of turning the tunnels into a complex and safe transport system.

Building the Tunnel was a huge job. Sizewell B nuclear power station and Canary Wharf were under construction at the same time, suggesting that skill and labour shortages might lead to cost increases. In the event, however, labour relations were not a major problem.

During construction there were many delays and arguments

concerning the nature and scope of the project; and lack of trust made things much worse. Eurotunnel wanted 'optimisation' – the best possible project for the price – and expected to review all engineering decisions, while holding TML responsible for costs. But when they started to issue instructions, TML regarded them as changes for which they would have to pay.

Clause 67 of the contract governing settlement of disputes referred them to a panel of experts. Meanwhile TML had to continue working even if Eurotunnel withheld payments. In the end, when TML sued Eurotunnel, the French courts ruled that Eurotunnel should pay TML £60 million a month – which the company did not have.

Alastair Morton of Eurotunnel was famous for brinkmanship and bullying. He enraged the constructors by briefing the press while holding TML to its contractual agreement to remain silent. From January 1988 Eurotunnel built up a Project Implementation Division, at its peak comprising 350 staff, thereby duplicating TML's project management function. TML accused Eurotunnel of 'day-to-day meddling', while Eurotunnel criticised TML for slow tunnelling.

The IGC and the Safety Authority quickly got involved in detailed issues relating to design features and safety standards, many with cost implications. For example, fire safety was a major worry, especially after the King's Cross fire of November 1987. The original requirement was for fire doors at the end of each shuttle car, which could close in the event of fire. This would hold back any blaze for 30 minutes and let passengers move to adjacent cars or the service tunnel.

But Eurotunnel promised that the wagons themselves would provide fire resistance of 30 minutes, to enable the whole train to clear the tunnel. This was more difficult – and more expensive. It required using new alloys, which made the cars much heavier. They then needed special locomotives with six motor axles instead of four: this in turn increased the power requirements.

By July 1989 the cost of the shuttle fleet had nearly tripled, from £220 million to £600 million, owing mainly to extra safety requirements. In 1990 production had to stop because, after a long dispute, the Safety Authority had insisted on increasing the width of pass doors by … 10 centimetres. The decision cost £40 million and months of delay. Eurotunnel had to bear the extra costs because the governments had exempted themselves from any financial risk.

The signalling system had to control 100 mph trains running three minutes apart and be able to stop a train automatically in case of danger. This being part of the lump-sum contract, there was a strong incentive for TML to keep costs low. But SNCF wanted a leading-edge system that it would be using for the high-speed link to Paris. So Eurotunnel *ordered* TML to award the contract to GEC-Alsthom for the system they were developing for SNCF. The other three bidders promptly sued TML, and the result was a huge increase in the cost of the signalling system.

Reducing the trains' speed in the tunnel made it possible to downgrade the expensive ventilation system. But the rolling stock was unreliable. The initial estimate for fourteen Eurostar Class 373 train sets was £230 million; but in December 1989 BR authorised spending of £356 million, an increase of 55 per cent. And the trains (sourced from seventeen different factories) were delivered over a year late. The Commons Transport Committee was highly critical: 'We cannot be the only ones to view with incredulity the fact that a Channel Tunnel can be built in less time than it takes to order and deliver the 34 trains which are to run through it.'[14]

The initial 1985 proposal (see Table 8) showed total construction costs for the Tunnel at £2,350 million (**£5,000 million**). (In addition Eurotunnel would have to bear corporate and other expenses and net financing costs.) Early tunnelling difficulties raised estimates of the project's cost and there were many problems with equipment and with terminal design. By late 1989 construction costs were forecast to total £4,700 million (**£8,000 million**). Upon completion in 1994, actual construction costs for the Channel Tunnel (excluding the high-speed link to London) turned out to be **£9,350 million**.[15] This was a cost overrun of **£4,350 million** (87 per cent).

Table 8 **Channel Tunnel construction costs: actual versus estimate**

2007 £ million Construction costs (see note 15)	Original Sept. '85	Actual May '94	Overrun £m	Overrun %
Tunnelling	2,300	4,300	2,000	87
Terminals	850	1,150	300	35
Fixed equipment	1,350	2,450	1,100	81
Rolling stock	500	1,450	950	190
Total	5,000	9,350	4,350	87

Eventually, after many expensive and time-consuming arguments, TML handed over the Tunnel to Eurotunnel in December 1993. TML's CEO reckoned[16] the losses of the ten constructing companies on the contract may have totalled between £600

---

14   Gourvish, op. cit., p. 326.

15   Based on ibid., pp. 320, 368.

16   Fetherston, op. cit., p. 386.

million and £800 million (say **£1,000 million**). Eurotunnel then had to commission the Tunnel themselves so that trains could begin to run through it. The Tunnel finally opened in May 1994, about twelve months late (and after another five UK transport ministers). The full passenger service did not begin until December 1994.

The two governments largely stood aloof during the difficult Tunnel construction process, but in order to help without cash subsidies, they extended Eurotunnel's concession period (55 years from 1987). In 1993 the Conservative government increased it by ten years, then in 1997 the Labour government extended it further to 99 years (in each case, of course, in agreement with the French government). At the end of the concession period, ownership of the Tunnel would revert to the British and French governments.

Customer demand

Eurotunnel's two largest direct customers were to be the state-owned railway companies BR and SNCF. The Railway Usage Contract of May 1987 arranged terms. They would run freight and passenger trains through the Tunnel and construct and manage the 'links' from the Tunnel to London and Paris. Eurotunnel would run its own heavy goods vehicles and tourist shuttles between its two terminals.

BR and SNCF agreed to provide infrastructure and rolling stock. They would also pay specified tolls (both fixed and variable) plus a proportion of the Tunnel's running costs. All this in return for half the Tunnel's capacity: it was to be able to carry 17.4 million passengers and 8.1 million tonnes of freight a year. Half of

Eurotunnel's revenues were expected to come from the railways, the other half from road vehicles.

In 1987 the parties agreed a Minimum Usage Charge (MUC). This was to help reassure Eurotunnel investors. It comprised a flat payment of £100 million a year (at 1985 prices [**£200 million**]) for twelve years from 1994. Everyone assumed that the actual toll payments, based on usage, would be higher. Indeed, Eurotunnel claimed 'there is no significant risk of [the fee] not being completely offset by the actual tolls'. But in the event, traffic was much lower than forecast, so the effect was to transfer some of the business risk from Eurotunnel to BR and SNCF (both then still state-owned). Without the MUC, Eurotunnel's results would have been even worse. But from late 2006, Eurotunnel started to receive much lower revenues based on actual traffic, instead of on the fixed 'minimum usage' charge.

Eurotunnel expected to have a competitive advantage over existing cross-Channel services such as ferries and hovercraft and airline services between major cities. It would be less vulnerable to bad weather and offer more frequent services. Also, journey times would be much shorter: just over an hour for Eurotunnel (from the UK's M20 to France's A26) compared with two hours for hovercraft and three hours for ferries. Apart from the speed advantage, the through trains would also be more convenient and more comfortable.

In France SNCF was proposing a new high-speed railway line between Paris and Brussels with a branch to Eurotunnel's French terminal. This would allow the new passenger trains to travel at speeds of up to 200 mph. There were also planned improvements to tracks on the UK side. These would ultimately lead to fast direct rail services between London and Paris (two and a quarter hours).

Compared with this, using existing trains with a ferry took seven hours, with hovercraft five and a half hours, while air travel took about three hours.

A market research study concluded that Eurotunnel was economically feasible. It predicted that between 1985 and 2003, cross-Channel passenger and freight traffic would double, and expected Eurotunnel to capture a large proportion of this growing market. Eurotunnel would require no pre-booking (it was introduced from 1996) and would rival airline services in terms of cost and time. The study predicted that in its first full year, Eurotunnel would carry 30 million passengers and 15 million tonnes of freight. The French numbers for the Channel Tunnel were consistently higher than the British, possibly because BR was not very keen on the project.

In the event, the growth of total cross-Channel traffic, both for passengers and freight, was greatly overestimated, whether by Eurotunnel itself, or by consultants, civil servants or academics.[17] One likely reason is the failure so far to complete the high-speed link from London to the Tunnel. The Tunnel did achieve its expected share of the market for passengers and bettered it for freight. After the opening of the Tunnel, passenger traffic grew rapidly until the ending of duty-free goods in 1998, after which it started to decline.

The following table[18] compares actual traffic in 2003 with forecasts made in 1987:

---

17   R. Anguera, 'The Channel Tunnel: an ex post economic evaluation', *Transportation Research*, vol. 40A, May 2006, pp. 291–315.

18   Calculated from Gourvish, op. cit., p. 370.

Table 9 **Channel Tunnel traffic: 2003 actual versus 1987 forecast**

	2003 traffic		*Shortfall v. 1987 forecast*	
Millions	*1987 forecast*	*Actual*	*Numbers*	*%*
Eurostar passengers	21.4	6.3	15.1	70
Total passengers (including shuttle)	39.5	14.7	24.8	63
Freight (tonnes)	21.1	13.3	7.8	37

But the overall results were very disappointing. For example, 15.9 million passengers had been predicted on the Eurostar trains in the opening year. But actual traffic in 1995, the first full year, was 2.9 million passengers, only 18 per cent of the forecast. The actual number of passengers in 2003 was more than 60 per cent below the 1987 forecasts. Another big surprise was a price war with the ferries and the failure to predict the success of the low-cost airlines, such as easyJet and Ryanair, which resulted in actual fares being some 40 per cent lower than in Eurotunnel's forecasts. With respect to freight, 'Eurotunnel's updates during the construction assumed an increasing total market, and that the Tunnel would capture a reduced share – the opposite to what actually happened.'[19]

The Channel Tunnel Rail Link (CTRL) to London

Alastair Morton made it clear that he expected the rail provision for the Tunnel to include a high-speed passenger service between London and Paris,[20] though it was not legally part of the deal (as it had been for the earlier Channel Tunnel project). A 1985 report

19   Anguera, op. cit., p. 299.
20   Gourvish, op. cit., p. 294.

to Kent County Council said the rail lines to London were already very heavily used; but at that time BR believed the existing rail network in the south-east could cope with any extra international traffic after the Tunnel opened. However, 1988 traffic forecasts suggested a need to increase rail capacity in the south-east as soon as the Tunnel opened, and BR thought constructing a new route was the best way to do this.

In November 1985 fixed works and rolling stock for BR's preferred high-speed option were costed at **£850 million**. Nicholas Ridley, the transport minister, insisted that any infrastructure investment BR might undertake in support of the project must be fully commercial.[21] And Mrs Thatcher herself said that users of the new line should pay for the full costs, including environmental costs. So it was *not* 'always envisaged that the Link would not be commercially viable without a substantial government financial contribution'.[22] Indeed, Section 42 of the Treaty explicitly ruled out government grants in support of international services.

By the summer of 1987 there had been a large increase in costs, and BR split the project into three parts: Phase I (**£900 million**), to meet the terms of the Usage Contract; Phase II (**£500 million**), for through services north of London, which the first proposals did not include; and Phase III (**£400 million**), for increasing line capacity and upgrading infrastructure. Omitting the new Ashford station and Phase II, for the time being, reduced the total cost to **£1,100 million**. But by July 1990 the Phase I cost alone had further increased to **£2,100 million**.

There were arguments about the precise route between

---

21   Ibid., pp. 256, 259, 287, 308, 336.

22   As stated in National Audit Office (NAO), *The Channel Tunnel Rail Link*, Report by Comptroller and Auditor General, HC 302 Session 2000/01, 28 March 2001, p. 6.

London and the Tunnel. There was also a need for a second station in addition to Waterloo. BR preferred a southerly route via Swanley and thence in tunnels to King's Cross. But in the end, even though it would cost £680 million (**£1,000 million**) more, the government decided on an easterly route via Thurrock and Stratford to St Pancras. A major reason was to avoid 'Nimby' ('not in my backyard') protests in marginal constituencies in Kent. Bob Reid, the BR chairman, was furious. He said it would 'take commuters where they don't want to go and add up to twenty minutes to their overall journeys'.

More than one study showed there was no business case for the CTRL project, but – like the Channel Tunnel itself – it was a vital element of the high-speed London–Paris railway. Also, there were environmental benefits and 'the government saw the project as one of national prestige'.[23] Without any government subsidy, BR's CTRL project would not pay its way. But the Channel Tunnel Treaty ruled out a government subsidy *only* for the state-owned BR, not for a *private sector* CTRL project!

So in 1990 BR studied a CTRL joint venture with EuroRail, drawing revenue mainly from Eurostar trains, but it required too much government money. There was much discussion lasting several years; but finally the government proposed a Private Finance Initiative project to design, build, finance and operate a high-speed rail link between the Tunnel and London. In February 1996 the winner was London & Continental Railways (LCR), a private consortium. There were competing claims for other major transport projects, such as the Jubilee Line extension and Cross-Rail, but the government agreed to contribute £1,700 million

---

23   Ibid., p. 7.

(**£2,400 million**) to a CTRL project costing £2,700 million. In all, with the transfer of public rail and land to LCR, the Labour opposition reckoned total public support was as high as £5,700 million[24] (**£7,700 million**).

The CTRL was to extend for 70 miles from the Tunnel to St Pancras station, via Stratford in East London. It would cut the journey time from London to Paris (and from London to Brussels) by 25 minutes, to 2 hours 15 minutes and 1 hour 50 minutes respectively. But a new station at Ebbsfleet 34 miles to the north will supersede the **£100 million** Eurostar station at Ashford, opened in 1996; just as Eurostar's Waterloo terminal will close when St Pancras opens.

In January 1998 LCR asked for a further £1,200 million of support, which the government refused. Instead the CTRL would be financed by a complex mixture of public and private finance and government guarantees. During this period, BR was privatised and its successor Railtrack's subsequent collapse further upset the arrangements. But the government did agree to provide up to **£1,000 million** of support to underpin Eurostar operations and to guarantee £3,750 million of LCR debt, in order to reduce interest costs. The government wanted to keep the project off the public sector balance sheet. But in 2006 the Office of National Statistics ruled[25] that LCR was so closely linked to government that the company's entire £5,000 million debt should count as part of the public sector debt.

Section I of the CTRL, 46 miles from the Tunnel to Fawkham Junction, in North Kent, cost **£2,250 million**, and opened in September 2003. Section II, 24 miles from Southfleet to St Pancras,

24   Gourvish, op. cit., p. 380.
25   *Financial Times*, 15 November 2006.

costing **£3,500 million**, is due to open in November 2007 – about a year late and thirteen and a half years (and at least a further nine transport ministers) after the Channel Tunnel itself opened. The total direct cost amounts to **£5,750 million**, of which probably at least **£3,000 million** has been borne by the government.

Conclusion

Building and running the Channel Tunnel has been ruinous for Eurotunnel. Total costs of construction, including equipment, were nearly twice as much as forecast, owing to delays and design changes. Without Alastair Morton's energy and focus, things might well have been even worse. Lack of trust between Eurotunnel, the constructors and the banks made a challenging task much more difficult. The Safety Authority had no incentive to care about costs, so its insistence on 'safety' at any cost proved very expensive.

When the Tunnel opened, passenger demand was less than half the forecast level, partly because there was no high-speed rail link to London, and freight traffic was down on forecast by more than a third. Budget airlines reduced air fares and attracted passenger business and, together with ferries' lower prices, reduced the price of travel far below Eurotunnel's forecasts. Financial gearing was very high for such a risky project: there was never enough financial 'slack', so Eurotunnel was on the verge of bankruptcy from the start. The promoters also failed to build a drive-through tunnel, though everyone soon forgot this 'promise', which may have helped get the concession in the first place.

Mrs Thatcher (together with President Mitterrand) insisted that private enterprise finance the Channel Tunnel itself; and both

British and French governments deserve credit for sticking to this decision. But the British government did not fulfil the requirement for the Channel Tunnel rail link to London to be 'fully commercial'. Neither the government nor BR gave enough priority to the CTRL, which was still not complete more than a dozen years after the Tunnel opened. It was a vital part of the Channel Tunnel project, to enable the railways to compete with the airlines on travel time.

The CTRL's cost was extremely high. So one way or another, the government had to provide probably at least **£3,000 million** to subsidise it, out of total costs of at least **£5,750 million**. Lack of transparency makes it very hard to measure the CTRL's total costs or the government's total contribution towards it. But compared with the implied target of zero government spending for a 'fully commercial' project, this clearly represents a significant cost overrun. Hence the entire Channel Tunnel project must rank as a 'government disaster'.

Acronyms

BR	British Rail
CTG–FM	Channel Tunnel Group–France Manche
CTRL	Channel Tunnel Rail Link (to London)
EIB	European Investment Bank
IGC	Inter-Governmental Commission
LCR	London and Continental Railways
MUC	Minimum Usage Charge
NAO	National Audit Office
SNCF	Société Nationale des Chemins de Fer Français
TBM	Tunnel-boring Machine
TML	TransManche-Link

7 THE MILLENNIUM DOME (1995–2000– …)

The Conservative years (1994–April 1997)

In February 1994 John Major's Conservative government set up a commission to oversee Millennium events, which the new National Lottery would finance. The Act said: 'The Millennium Commission shall not be regarded as the servant or agent of the Crown'; but in fact it was the government's creature. In June its chairman suggested a Millennium Exhibition to open on New Year's Eve and run through the whole of the year 2000. (The new millennium would actually begin on 1 January 2001, but most people regarded insistence on that fact as pedantry.) There was no great public enthusiasm, and many commissioners were against the idea, but the politicians were clearly keen.

This Millennium Exhibition would somewhat resemble two earlier national events which both ran for about five summer months in central London. The Great Exhibition of 1851, in the Crystal Palace in Hyde Park, was open from May to mid-October, had more than six million paying visitors – and made a profit. The 1951 Festival of Britain, costing £11 million (**£250 million**), ran on the South Bank from May to September, with 8.5 million visitors. (There had also been the British Empire Exhibition of 1924/25 at Wembley.)

In May 1995 the Commission's guidelines for sites wishing

to host the exhibition suggested planning for up to a hundred thousand visitors a day: 'As a minimum it is envisaged that the exhibition will attract 15 million people, [but] a figure in excess of 30 million is unlikely …'[1] This suggests that the politicians were extremely ambitious from the start. Fifteen million visitors in a year would imply an *average* of more than forty thousand people every day.

Fifty-seven sites applied, but by the autumn it was a straight fight between Birmingham and Greenwich in south-east London. Birmingham would use a 16-acre site near the National Exhibition Centre close to the M6 and M42. It had its own train station and airport and extensive parking, and 30 million people lived within two hours' travel. Moreover, it claimed expertise in large-scale event management. The London-based company Imagination had drawn up designs using ten pavilions with time themes.

The bleak Greenwich peninsula contained a derelict and contaminated gasworks. Greenwich had the 'advantage' of being on the meridian line, but road and rail access were poor, and there was little or no infrastructure. There was very limited parking space, but London Underground was building a 10-mile extension to the Jubilee Line from Green Park through Docklands to Stratford. (British Gas had paid London Underground £20 million to route the Jubilee Line Extension through the Greenwich peninsula, crossing the river twice.) The new station at North Greenwich would offer easy access – if it was open in time. Choosing Greenwich would also offer the chance to create 10,000 jobs in an area of high unemployment and urban decay.

Meanwhile the Commission, which always expected to make a

---

1   National Audit Office (NAO), *The Millennium Dome*, Report by Comptroller and Auditor General, HC 936, Session 1999/2000 (Report 1), 9 November 2000, p. 39.

substantial grant from National Lottery funds, was also looking at private sector bids to organise and run the event. The task would be to conceive, design, construct, manage, finance, market and operate the exhibition for the whole of the year 2000 on a single site. Some people believed that the decision to separate choice of site from choice of operator was a mistake that delayed the whole project by a year. In October, out of sixteen potential organisers, four were shortlisted. Granada dropped out, leaving the MAI consortium, run by Lord Hollick; M2000, headed by Touche Ross; and Imagination, led by Gary Withers. When MAI linked up with M2000, they were down to two.

In January 1996 the Commission was 'greatly impressed by the exciting vision and concept' submitted by Imagination for Birmingham. It invited them to develop proposals for *both* sites. In response, the company proposed twelve time-based pavilions for Greenwich. On 28 February the Commission announced that it had decided to base the project at Greenwich, using Imagination's outline concepts. Although nobody realised it at the time, that decision – which government ministers had heavily influenced – meant that this would be a *government* project.

It soon became obvious that building twelve substantial and separate pavilions would be too expensive. So the concept of a single-span dome emerged, providing a 'cost-effective solution to the requirement to keep visitors warm and dry on a windy peninsula …' At first the structure was to be temporary, but later the Labour government insisted on a permanent 'legacy' building.

In early June Michael Heseltine called a meeting of potential sponsors to hear about the Dome's design concept and to drum up commitment. He was deputy prime minister, a strong supporter of the project, and a Millennium Commissioner throughout. The government was very worried about costs spiralling above £500 million. Partly to reassure sponsors, it announced that if necessary it would extend the Millennium Commission's life beyond 31 December 2000. That would legally enable it to receive further National Lottery money to bail out the exhibition's expected losses, and amounted to an unwritten government guarantee. This was an explicit link between government and lottery grants.

A new company, Millennium Central Ltd, was set up to run the project. In September, Barry Hartop became acting chief executive, with Robert Ayling, of British Airways, as chairman. Commercial partners were sought, but without success: there were just too many uncertainties. There was no property developer for Greenwich, no exhibition operator and there were no investors.

In October 1996 Andrew Turnbull, the Department of the Environment's Permanent Secretary, questioned the value of spending public funds to purchase such a contaminated site at that time; but the government overruled him. In November British Gas agreed to transfer ownership of the entire 294-acre Greenwich peninsula site to English Partnerships, the government's Urban Regeneration Agency. One hundred and thirty acres were earmarked for the Millennium Exhibition. The total cost to government of the investment, including acquisition of the site (£20 million) together with clearing and decontamination and providing new roads and services and landscaping, amounted to £200 million (**£250 million**). Friends of the Earth objected, believing the polluter – British Gas – should have paid for the clean-up.

In December Barry Hartop presented the overall business plan, showing that total costs had increased to over £700 million. But the Millennium Commission rejected the plan and he left the project soon afterwards. There was a radical review of the project's costs. The press had always been sceptical, partly because the first lottery grant had been £12 million to the Churchill family for Winston Churchill's state papers. Now the media became positively hostile.

A general election was due within six months, with the Conservative government likely to lose it. For that reason it was important for the Opposition to have at least one nominee on the Commission (the government had two ministers on it). Mrs Bottomley, the National Heritage Secretary, said she had always tried to keep the Millennium Exhibition non-party. So it was a nasty shock when Jack Cunningham, her shadow, said: 'I am not giving a blank cheque on behalf of the Labour party.' She later claimed that these and other comments discouraged early sponsorship.

In January 1997, the Commission announced a £200 million grant (**£250 million**) from lottery funds towards the costs of the exhibition at Greenwich (in addition to regeneration). They also said: '[We have] a target of £150 million for sponsorship, of which more than half has been identified. Entrance charges will be set at a level which allows as many people as possible to attend but which also maximises revenue.'[2] In addition it hoped to get £150 million from ticket sales and merchandising to visitors, implying total income of £500 million. The statement added: 'No public expenditure will be committed to the Exhibition beyond that … to English Partnerships to acquire and prepare the site.'[3]

---

2   It is not easy to see how one could maximise both numbers and revenue at the same time, since lower prices would be almost certain to increase numbers at least slightly.

3   Alastair Irvine, *The Battle for the Millennium Dome*, Irvine News Agency, 1999, p. 58. The government (unlike almost everyone else) did not regard lottery money as 'public expenditure'.

It had now become obvious that no private company would accept the risks of mounting the event, even with a substantial grant from lottery funds. But the politicians were reluctant to abandon the project. Instead the Conservative government decided that a public sector company should run the exhibition, its sole shareholder being a minister. Millennium Central Ltd became the first private sector company to be nationalised since the 1970s. The Chancellor of the Duchy of Lancaster, Roger Freeman, became the Shareholder instead of the National Heritage Secretary, who remained chairman of the Millennium Commission.

In February Jennie Page was appointed as the company's chief executive. She had formerly been chief executive of the Millennium Commission and before that head of English Heritage, which was responsible for regeneration (on the Greenwich peninsula among many other places). She had a good knowledge of how Whitehall works, which was important in such a political project. Almost at once the company issued a totally new content brief for the Dome.

As a result, in March, Imagination withdrew from the project. That design company lacked the experience to take the lead in such an enormous project and failed to control costs. They complained of constant changes to the budget and business plan, which created delays in the timetable. Mrs Bottomley later commented: 'I always regarded the project rather like the Channel Tunnel or many other great ventures. They are fraught with tension and uncertainty and argument all the way until completion and then they tend to be a spectacular success.'[4] But the first Channel Tunnel project had been cancelled by a newly elected

---

4   Ibid., p. 61.

Labour government (in 1975). Would the same thing happen to the Millennium Dome a generation later?

The Labour years (from May 1997)

In May 1997 a Labour government came to power. The Department of National Heritage was renamed the Department for Culture, Media and Sport (CMS), and Chris Smith replaced Virginia Bottomley as secretary of state. Most of the new cabinet, including him, were sceptical about the total cost of the Dome. Smith was also appalled at the lack of detail about what would actually go inside the structure. Many Labour MPs were in favour of scrapping the whole project.

The Labour government certainly considered abandoning the Dome, having serious worries both about the management and about its finances. The piling contract had been arranged before there was a decision about the Dome's future, but the piledrivers themselves would need to start on-site no later than 23 June. So the new government had to make a go/no go decision almost at once.

Tony Blair, the prime minister, was in favour of the project, as was John Prescott, the deputy prime minister. So on 19 June the cabinet decided that the Millennium Exhibition should go ahead. Peter Mandelson, minister without portfolio, was put in charge, as the Shareholder of Millennium Central Ltd, with Chris Smith as chairman of the Millennium Commission. That same day, all four of them, together with Michael Heseltine, visited the site to demonstrate publicly the government's backing for the project.

But there were five requirements for the exhibition:

- The Dome must provide a lasting legacy.

- There must be no extra cost to the public purse.
- The content must entertain and inspire.
- It must relate to the whole nation (not just London and the south-east).
- There must be a new management structure to provide a greater creative force.

Mandelson certainly faced some urgent challenges. There were four main tasks: to build the Dome, define the content, get the sponsorship, and sell the tickets. In July the company changed its name to New Millennium Experience Company Ltd (NMEC). The name clearly implied that the celebrations were looking forward to the 'new' millennium, rather than backwards at the old one. An immediate problem was that Jennie Page, as NMEC's chief executive, was strongly objecting to the very terms that she herself, as chief executive of the Millennium Commission, had earlier been proposing for the grant to Millennium Central Ltd.![5]

Construction of the Dome itself was completed by June 1998. It had a circumference of more than half a mile, and a maximum height of 50 yards. The ground-floor area was nearly 100,000 square yards, big enough to hold 18,000 Routemaster buses. The roof fabric was a problem: polyester coated with PVC would be cheaper, but woven glass-fibre coated with Teflon would last longer. After first choosing PVC ('the safest and strongest option'), Mandelson changed his mind and approved the more expensive option. The new fabric cost £8 million more and added three months to the design programme. The biggest crane in Europe was hired to raise the huge masts.

5   Adam Nicolson, *Regeneration*, HarperCollins, London, 1999, p. 120.

Since Imagination had withdrawn from the project, nobody knew what was going inside the Dome. Just before the election Stephen Bayley had been recruited as Consultant Creative Director. Afterwards he claimed that NMEC was dominated by 'public sector mentality'. 'They simply wanted to *say* they had a creative director. They didn't actually want one.'[6] Bayley saw his role as being in charge of commissioning the work for the zones and developing their design, direction and intellectual content. The relationship between him and Mandelson started badly and rapidly got worse. He resigned in January 1998.

Imagination's designs had cost £7.6 million, with twenty detailed versions of their proposals, but Mandelson said he inherited a 'blank sheet' of ideas. By the summer of 1997, there was public clamour to know what the Dome would contain. The *Observer* called it 'a vacuum held together by rhetoric'. The *Sunday Times* said: 'There was nothing wrong with the idea of a memorial to celebrate the end of the millennium: the problem was that the Dome was too grandiose and lacking in purpose.' On 17 December the CMS Select Committee issued a report saying: 'At times the process of discovering the proposals for the content of the Dome was akin to drawing teeth. From what we know so far, the Millennium Experience is not so much a journey through time as … a journey into the unknown.'[7] In particular, was it meant to be entertainment or educational, an amusement park or a trade fair?

The project suffered a major blow in December when NMEC decided to drop Sir Cameron Mackintosh's ambitious proposals for a theatrical show inside the Dome. It had been going to cost more than £200 million! Press criticism became even worse

6   Ibid., p. 169.
7   Irvine, op. cit., p. 81.

than before. It was no help that Peter Mandelson was probably the least trusted politician in the country. He asked the Shadow Cabinet to stop knocking the Dome – very much the same plea that Virginia Bottomley had made to Tony Blair a year earlier. She had claimed a Labour pre-election dirty tricks campaign, orchestrated by Mandelson, was threatening the project and discouraging sponsors.

Companies were reluctant to sign up as sponsors before they knew what the content would be. In February 1998, BT, Manpower, Sky and Tesco became 'founding partners', pledging at least £12 million each. Others, such as BA, BAA, Camelot and the Corporation of London, came in with smaller amounts. A total of £75 million was announced, but it was not clear how definite it was. There were two major problems: ensuring that sponsors paid in cash, not in kind, and the lack of a standard set of rules for sponsorship. On some zones the agreement between NMEC and the sponsors went through more than fifty drafts![8]

In December 1998 a scandal over a loan from a government colleague, which he had failed to include in the register of members' interests, forced Mandelson to resign. His successor as Shareholder was Lord Falconer, of the Cabinet Office.

The final year was a race against time, both for sponsors and for Dome content. Few zones were finished before the very last week of 1999. With the Dome contents so obscure, and with the hostile media, it was very hard to sell tickets in advance during 1999 as had been planned. Of the visitors to Greenwich, four-fifths were expected to travel by Underground, one fifth by bus. The Jubilee Line Extension, costing £3,250 million (**£4,000 million**),

---

8   Nicolson, op. cit., p. 205.

had been due to take under three years to complete, but eventually took nearly five years. It finally opened only a few weeks before the Dome itself.

Organisation

The pattern of responsibilities for the Dome was somewhat complex.[9] NMEC was in charge of running the Dome. It was accountable both to the Shareholder (the government) and to the Millennium Commission, which was providing grant aid from lottery funds; and in effect to CMS, which was advising both. Almost all NMEC's directors were non-executive and unpaid. There were regular directors' meetings, which the Shareholder, CMS and the Commission attended on occasion.

The Shareholder:
- appointed directors, and agreed their terms of employment;
- controlled the company by means of a financial memorandum;
- answered to Parliament for NMEC's performance;
- monitored progress against five key government commitments made in 1997, covering cost, content, national impact, effective management, and post-2000.

CMS:
- advised the secretary of state and the Shareholder;
- issued policy and financial directions for lottery bodies such as the Commission;

---

9   Summarised from NAO Report 1, op. cit., p. 7.

- advised the Shareholder about adherence to the financial memorandum (under which the department's Permanent Secretary could issue instructions to NMEC).

The Commission's function was to grant-aid projects, not to run projects itself. The Secretary of State for CMS was chairman.

The Commission:
- made lottery grants to NMEC;
- held the company accountable for its use of the Commission's grants, by means of a grant memorandum setting out the terms and conditions;
- approved the company's business plans and budgets;
- monitored NMEC's progress in building and running the Dome.

The opening night

The opening night on New Year's Eve (which cost £5 million) was something of a disaster. It is hard to tell whether this stemmed from management incompetence or whether it was just bad luck. NMEC invited 10,000 special guests, but owing to a planning error many of the guests' admission tickets were not sent out in time. So it was decided to issue the tickets at the Underground stations. The politicians and their entourage would travel from Westminster, while newspaper editors, journalists, sponsors and their families were to pick up their tickets at Stratford station in north-east London.

But the new station at Stratford was ill equipped to handle such a big crowd. As a result 3,000 invitees queued for up to four hours, first for security checks, then for admission tickets and finally for Underground trains. When they eventually reached the Dome, many had missed the celebration, including prominent newspaper editors and the BBC's director-general. Dominic Lawson, editor of the *Sunday Telegraph*, noted: 'Nobody knew what was going on and the announcements were completely unhelpful ... By the time people got there some of the Zones had been shut down ...'

The opening-night fiasco provoked the press to attack the Dome more fiercely than ever, criticising the queues, the content, equipment breakdowns and the management. All this discouraged demand. The sponsors too were upset about their zone problems, and threatened to withhold further payments until they were resolved.

Costs

The May 1997 'plan', with total costs of £758 million[10] (including £88 million contingencies), represented an increase of more than 50 per cent over the earlier estimate of £500 million. It resulted in the government's original lottery grant award of £449 million in July 1997. This comprised the initial £200 million plus £199 million 'shortfall' plus £50 million extra for working capital, repayable at the end. The actual costs were £789 million[11] (see Table 10).

---

10   Excluding £13 million which the Commission paid to consultants for development work prior to January 1997.

11   NAO, *Winding up NMEC*, Report by the Comptroller and Auditor General, HC 749, Session 2001/02 (Report 2), 17 April 2002, p. 23.

Table 10 **Millennium Dome costs: actual versus plan**

£ million	Plan	Actual	Difference
Dome site and structures*	309	301	−8
Infrastructure and transport	53	30	−23
Dome contents*	168	173	+ 5
Operations and marketing	144	161	+ 17
Payroll and corporate services	27	50	+ 23
National programme	57	45	−12
Decommissioning/close down	–	25	+ 25
Liquidation expenditure	–	4	+ 4
Total	758	789	+ 31

* After transferring £55 million from Dome contents to Dome site and structures.

Total spending was £31 million (4 per cent) up on the May 1997 plan, of which £29 million was to do with decommissioning/ closing down and liquidation (omitted from the earlier plan). Even comparing £789 million with the £670 million planned spending *excluding* £88 million cost contingencies, the increase is 'only' 18 per cent. This is not huge by the standards of the five other projects.

According to David James, however, 'the bought ledger at the Dome was a complete and utter catastrophe'.[12] Between March and June 2000 unexpected liabilities totalling more than £5 million came to light. As at 31 July 2000 some 60 per cent of outstanding invoices had been due for payment since before 31 March 2000.[13]

Customer demand

The Commission's staff had suggested basing the business plan,

---

12   House of Lords, 1 March 2007.

13   NAO Report 1, op. cit., pp. 9, 32.

for the sake of prudence, on 8 million (paying) visitors, the 'worst case' estimate from its consultants, Deloitte & Touche. But in the end the Commission accepted NMEC's plan assuming 12 million paying visitors. This meant the Dome would have to attract more than *four times* as many people as the next most popular 'pay-to-visit' place (Alton Towers) achieved in 1999. But NMEC's senior staff had no experience of running a large visitor attraction.

In 1997 there had been no final decisions on the Dome's contents, ticket prices, marketing strategies or whether there would be access to the area by car. So at that stage customer demand was uncertain, to put it mildly. The marketing team spent 90 per cent of their budget in the six months before the Dome opened. But the promotions could not explain what was inside the Dome because at that time the zones were not complete and most of the content was still unknown. (Even after the Dome was open, people who had visited it had difficulty describing the experience to others.) Weather in the early months would be poor; yet, in the absence of previous years, it would be hard to assess the impact of any seasonal influences. (In the event these seemed to be small.)

Camelot, the National Lottery operator, sold admission tickets at various outlets around London and the UK – but not at the Dome itself. Many visitors arrived at the Dome only to find they were unable to buy a ticket there. Instead they had to take the Underground or bus to the nearest outlet. In the early weeks people found that travel costs were high and travel times were long. Ticket prices were £20 per adult and £16.50 for children aged between five and fifteen. The original plan had been to sell tickets only in advance, but soon after the Dome opened NMEC started to sell tickets at the door, though the absence of turnstiles was a problem.

During 2000, NMEC revised downwards its forecasts of the number of paying visitors as follows:

On 28 January   from 12 million to 10 million
On 19 May   from 10 million to 6 million
In August   from 6 million to 4.5 million.

By September the company was planning for 4.5 million paying customers (6 million in total, including 1 million schoolchildren that NMEC had agreed to let in free), just over one third of the initial estimate. On a pro rata basis, this would cut revenue from tickets and merchandising from £169 million to £63 million. Actual numbers exceeded the September estimate, at 5.5 million paying customers, but total cash receipts from visitors were only £60 million.

Sources of funds

The project was to be funded from three sources:

- the National Lottery   £414 million[14]
- visitors (tickets and merchandising)   £169 million[15]
- commercial sponsors   £175 million[15]
                                                £758 million

The projections included total contingencies of £133 million: costs £88 million (13 per cent) and revenues £45 million – £25 million (13 per cent) for visitors and £20 million (10 per cent) for commercial sponsors. Neither provision was large enough.

14   = £200 million + £199 million shortfall + £15 million legacy costs.
15   Net of contingencies.

NMEC found it very hard to foresee the amount and timing of its funding needs for this unique attraction, while the Commission could not legally fund in advance of need, which was a recipe for trouble. The Dome's financial problems were due partly to the *timing* of cash in and out, but mainly to the serious income shortfall. In advance there was enormous pressure on containing costs, but in the event it was the *quality* of the spending, rather than the quantity, which turned out to be the main problem.

Once the Dome had been constructed, there was little room for manoeuvre in the face of the significant shortfall in visitor numbers. Closing the Dome early and liquidating NMEC would have made no sense, since most of the expenditure was already committed. The only options were either to try to increase receipts from visitors or (failing that) to get further grants from the Commission.

The May 1997 plan showed income from sponsors of £175 million and from visitors of £169 million. These amounts were £25 million and £19 million respectively *higher* than the estimates of only four months earlier (£150 million each).

At the end of 1999, just before the Dome opened, cash actually received from sponsors totalled £75 million (against £125 million planned by then), and cash received from advance ticket sales totalled only £4 million (against £19 million planned by then). So already cash flow was £65 million behind schedule. But a January 2000 revised budget showed revenue from visitors only £10 million down at £159 million. In the event, the costs were funded as shown in Table 11:[16]

---

16   Adapted from NAO Report 2, op. cit., pp. 23–4.

Table 11 **Millennium Dome revenues: actual versus plan**

£ million		Plan	Actual	Difference Money	%
Sponsors*		175	120	−55	−31
Visitors:	Tickets	136	54	− 82	−60
Visitors:	Retail & catering	33	6	− 27	−82
Sale of assets, etc.		−	9	+ 9	
Sale of Dome		15	−	−15	
Total revenues (ex. lottery grant)		359	189	−170	−47
Total costs		758	789	+ 31	
Net lottery grant		399	600	+ 201	
Grant surplus		50	25	−25	
Lottery grant		449	625†	+ 176	

*Income from sponsors: £85 million cash plus £35 million in kind.
†Actual grant £628 million owing to net £3 million spent on New Year opening.

In total non-government income was down by £170 million and total spending up by £31 million. So the initial estimate of a £200 million (**£250 million**) lottery grant, which later became £399 million (**£500 million**), increased to a need for £600 million (**£725 million**). That was in addition to the £200 million (**£250 million**) cost to government of acquiring and cleaning up the Greenwich peninsula site. The lottery grant was nearly three times as much as originally proposed. (Lottery money is treated here as government money – as indeed the government itself seems to have treated it in practice.) It was 45 per cent higher than expected in 1997, not because costs were much higher, but mainly because income was much less than planned – from sponsors, ticket sales and merchandising.

Operations

Once the Dome opened, there was daily pressure from sponsors, a huge cash shortfall, contractors screaming for payment and many fewer visitors than expected. In addition there was constant negative media coverage and low staff morale. So the Commission agreed to further funding only if NMEC brought in more management expertise. This led to Jennie Page, a civil servant with no experience of managing an attraction like the Dome, resigning just five weeks after the opening.

In her place they hired P. Y. Gerbeau, a former French Olympic hockey player who had spent ten years as a vice-president at Disneyland Paris. As soon as PY (as he was known) arrived on 7 February,[17] there was a rapid shake-up of top managers: the directors of entertainment and maintenance left at once. The executive team shrank from twenty to seven and moved from Buckingham Palace Road (SW1) to three newly acquired Portakabins at the Dome site (SE10).

In early February there were several serious problems: inadequate signage, stuck escalators and faulty equipment in nearly every zone. And there were long queues despite the number of visitors being far fewer than expected. On weekends a two-and-a-half-hour queue for the popular Body Zone near the entrance made it hard for other people to get past. Because of technical problems, one in five of the fifty-minute Millennium Shows had to be cancelled. The map of the Dome had been printed upside down, so visitors had great trouble finding out where they were. On top of all this, there was almost no money to fix the problems.

---

17 Many details in this section come from the London Business School case study, 'PY and the Dome', LBS-CS01-002, April 2001.

It was no help that apparently[18] a government rule said that if you had already used a particular consultant successfully you were not allowed to use the same consultant again.

A mixture of timed tickets, layout changes and improved signs reduced peak-time queues by 90 per cent from two and a half hours to fifteen minutes. PY combined two maintenance groups and introduced three levels of maintenance: preventive, reactive and crisis. He aimed to find £20 million of cost savings on things that would not affect sales.

The Commission would not allow him to reduce prices to increase volume, but selling tickets at the gate increased sales by 20 per cent. An e-mail campaign aimed at Americans led to 250,000 visitors. In early summer a £1 million promotion campaign led to 1 million enquiries and 450,000 direct ticket sales.

NMEC outsourced food service but owned and managed all the Dome merchandise outlets. The shops were poorly designed and sales of merchandise in January yielded only £2.30 per person. There were very limited sales of the collectable items. During the year retail income from shops amounted to only £2 million against a budget of £24 million. The NAO said there were far too many product lines (2,500) and too few points of sale. Catering income was also well down on plan.

Grants during the year

Given NMEC's severe shortfall in revenue, the Millennium Commission approved four further cash grants[19] from lottery

---

18 David James, House of Lords, 1 March 2007.

19 NAO Report 1, op. cit., p. 19. The government did not call these 'public expenditure', hence did not regard them as an 'extra cost to the public purse'.

funds during the year, totalling £179 million. In effect the company was on the verge of insolvency throughout the whole year the Dome was open. This was partly a question of the *timing* of cash flows, since costs were incurred before most income came in.

In February 2000 the Commission granted an extra £60 million, mainly because sponsorship income was down by £53 million, to £122 million. With 10 million paying visitors, instead of 12 million, projected ticket income, at £128 million, was only £8 million down on plan.

On 18 May NMEC said it would be unable to continue trading beyond 22 May. The next day it applied for a further grant of £39 million. This was based on 6 million paying visitors, with ticket income down a further £59 million; but sponsorship income was somewhat higher than projected in February. The 'worst case' forecast predicted a need for a further £80 million grant in due course. The Commission decided to grant only an extra £26 million plus a further £3 million to support extra marketing: it was concerned that the company had not fully examined options for cost-cutting.

The Commission chairman stated in Parliament on 12 June: 'I was delighted that … NMEC's Chief Executive confirmed last week that he would not return to the Millennium Commission for extra funds.' In June the NMEC board sought and received from CMS an indemnity against any wrongful trading action brought against them by creditors.

NMEC's chairman wrote to the Shareholder on 14 July, and to the Commission on 19 July, advising them of a further deterioration in finances. The Commission's own assessment was that the company might run out of money within two weeks and might require another £45 million. On 2 August NMEC applied for up to

£53 million on the basis of its expected share of the proceeds from the sale of the Dome. It was now assuming 4.75 million paying visitors. With a potential buyer of the Dome in view (although contracts had not yet been exchanged), the Commission agreed to grant a further £43 million.

On 4 August David James, an expert in company rescues, agreed to an unpaid assignment with NMEC, but only after PricewaterhouseCoopers reported on its solvency. On 29 August NMEC's chairman informed the Commission that the company was insolvent, and requested an extra £38 million (in addition to the recent £43 million). On 5 September the Commission, to facilitate the sale of the Dome, agreed to award the £38 million requested, plus another £9 million to cover liabilities likely to crystallise just before or after the planned sale of the Dome in the first quarter of 2001.

On 12 September discussions ended with Dome Europe regarding the sale of the Dome. The previous £47 million grant award had been to enable NMEC to proceed to a deal with Dome Europe, so that offer of grant lapsed. The next day the Commission agreed to award £47 million to the company to enable it to keep going until the end of the year: it would also assist the orderly rundown of NMEC in 2001 and safeguard the high-quality regeneration of the Greenwich peninsula.

Thus the four further cash grants in 2000 totalled £179 million:

February 2000	£60 million
22 May 2000	£29 million
August 2000	£43 million
5 September 2000	£47 million
	£179 million

In each of the four cases outlined above, the Commission's Accounting Officer had to consider whether these grants represented 'value for money'. On two occasions, in May and September, he concluded that he needed a written direction from the commissioners to pay the extra grant. Each such direction instructed him to make the payment in the light of wider considerations – 'the economic impact of premature closure' and 'the reputation of the UK'.[20] Quite what the latter referred to is unclear: perhaps it was a synonym for 'national prestige' (a 'benefit' also claimed for all the other projects).

After the millennium

It had been intended that at the end of 2000 the Dome would close and be sold. On 5 December 2000 ministers from two government departments[21] agreed to split any net proceeds from the sale. English Partnerships, the government's regeneration agency, owned the Dome site and granted NMEC a lease up to 30 June 2001. Thereafter, full responsibility for the land reverted to English Partnerships.

Over the next three years English Partnerships spent £15 million decommissioning the Dome's contents and managing and maintaining it, and another £15 million in costs related to the two sales – first to Dome Europe (backed by Nomura), then Legacy plc; and second to Meridian Delta Ltd (a joint venture between Quintain Estates and Lend Lease) and the Anschutz Entertainment

---

20 Ibid., p. 2.
21 The Department for Culture, Media and Sport for NMEC and the Department for the Environment, Transport and the Regions for English Partnerships.

Group.[22] In January 2007 it was announced that the country's first super-casino would be sited in Manchester and not at the Dome – whose future was thus once again in doubt.

Conclusion

The Millennium Dome was hardly a huge success, with many serious production and marketing shortcomings. Devising and producing the contents of each of the zones proved a real struggle. But the Dome did attract and largely satisfy 5.5 million paying visitors in the year 2000, though on-site sales per visitor and sponsorship support were much lower than expected.

Part of the reason for disappointment was that all the official hype set a target that was completely out of reach. The net cost[23] to government funds (including lottery money) was just over **£1,000 million**[24] compared with an original target of **£500 million** (increased in May 1997 to **£750 million**). Financial forecasting was very poor all through the year 2000, as well as earlier.

A number of people put in heroic efforts to make the Millennium Exhibition a success, including Michael Heseltine, Simon Jenkins, Jennie Page, Peter Mandelson and P. Y. Gerbeau. But the skills required to get such a project up and running turned out not to be the same as those needed to operate the Dome. There was

---

22 Report by the Comptroller and Auditor General, *English Partnerships: Regeneration of the Millennium Dome and Associated Land*, National Audit Office, HC 178 Session 2004/05 (Report 3), 12 January 2005.

23 Including regeneration of the Greenwich peninsula, without which, of course, there could have been no Dome.

24 Including the £30 million spent by English Partnerships on decommissioning, maintaining and trying to sell the Dome, as well as the £13 million spent pre-1997 by the Millennium Commission.

extensive political 'interference' throughout – but without it the Dome project would never have happened.

There were indeed many planning and operational problems. The opening-night fiasco got the Dome off to a dreadful start. In the early weeks there were multiple equipment breakdowns and very long queues. But the results could have been much worse if the original top management had remained in place. P. Y. Gerbeau, appointed at the end of February 2000, was a great success and fully deserved his £45,000 bonus at the end of the year. David James, who acted as unpaid executive chairman from September 2000, also fully earned his bonus of £100,000.

The failure to sell the Dome until three and a half years after the end of 2000 and its failure in 2007 to become the site of a super-casino were perhaps typical of the way so many aspects of the project went wrong.

Acronyms

CMS   (Department of) Culture, Media and Sport
NAO   National Audit Office
NMEC   New Millennium Experience Company

8 ASPECTS OF GOVERNMENT

Ministries

The 'government' is by no means monolithic. All six projects were complex enough to involve more than one department, in addition to the Treasury. Moreover, these days most British politicians regularly move about during their careers in government, so senior ministers usually have experience of several different departments. John Reid was exceptional in having served in as many as *nine* different departments in the ten years between 1997 and 2007; but so was Gordon Brown, who held only a single post over the same period.

As the Duchess of Omnium put it, in Trollope's *The Prime Minister*: 'You Ministers go on shuffling the old cards till they are so worn out and dirty that one can hardly tell the pips on them.' (To which the duke replied: 'I am one of the dirty old cards myself.') This is part of our 'generalist' tradition which critics sometimes deplore as 'amateur'. As a result, during a lengthy project, several different ministers may head the sponsoring department. The chance of a fresh viewpoint may offset any lack of continuity, though ministers often seem to 'go native' remarkably quickly.[1]

---

1   Jock Bruce-Gardyne and Nigel Lawson, *The Power Game: An Examination of Decision-making in Government*, Macmillan, Basingstoke, 1976, p. 159.

But perhaps it was *too much* of a good thing to have as many as 25 different ministers of transport between 1964 and 2003; or twenty different ministers of power or energy between 1955 and 1995; or eleven different ministers of aviation between 1959 and 1979. Such frequent changes produced an average period of less than two years per minister,[2] which suggests a danger that a 'new' minister is likely to move on just when he has almost mastered a department's most important topics. (There was only one woman in the three departments – Barbara Castle at Transport between December 1965 and April 1968.) This is illustrated by the very first episode of *Yes Minister*, which was 'fiction', but often painfully true to life. Jim Hacker, who had shadowed Agriculture for seven years in opposition, got a different department in government because the Permanent Secretary of Agriculture thought he was too 'genned up' on the subject!

Between 1966 and 1976, prime ministers Wilson and Heath were keen on reshuffling the *departments* themselves. Transport was mainly unchanged; but Aviation merged into Technology, became Aerospace, then part of Industry; while Power also merged into Technology, then Trade and Industry, then became Energy, then merged with Trade. It is not clear how much all this mattered. Feldman suggests[3] that in Concorde's case, at least, the relevant working team remained intact.

---

2 See Hugh Heclo and Aaron Wildavsky, *The Private Government of Public Money*, Macmillan, Basingstoke, 2nd edn, 1981, p. 130.

3 Elliot J. Feldman, *Concorde and Dissent: Explaining high technology failures in Britain and France*, Cambridge University Press, 1985, p. 140.

Project sponsors

R.101 airship

From January 1914 the army transferred all government airships to the Royal Navy. From October 1919, airships came under a separate Air Ministry, after a fierce debate about whether they should be the province of the Admiralty. The first chairman of the committee looking into the airships venture was Leo Amery, from the Admiralty, though his successor, Sir Samuel Hoare, was the air minister. Even inside the Air Ministry there was a contrast between those in the Royal Airship Works at Cardington, who had experience of lighter-than-air airships, and most of those in London and elsewhere, who knew only heavier-than-air aeroplanes.

The groundnut scheme

It was a surprise in October 1946 for the Ministry of Food to be asked to oversee the groundnut scheme. It must have been awkward for that ministry to manage a huge project in the single largest area the Colonial Office controlled. Moreover, launching a *mechanised* project meant completely reversing the traditional policy of preserving native ways of life. In 1951 a new Minister of Food recognised that the large-scale groundnut scheme had clearly failed. Only then did the Colonial Office take charge of the much-reduced enterprise.

Nuclear power

Oversight of the Central Electricity Generating Board (CEGB) began with the Ministry of Fuel and Power, from 1955 to 1969; then moved to the Ministry of Technology, then to the Department of

Trade and Industry (DTI), then from 1974 until privatisation to the Ministry of Energy. The Secretary of State for Scotland supervised the South of Scotland Electricity Board (SSEB). Oversight of the Atomic Energy Authority (AEA) rested from 1954 with a senior minister otherwise unconcerned with atomic energy. From 1964 the Minister of Technology was responsible; and from 1969 the same minister as oversaw the CEGB. The Secretary of State for the Environment, concerned about safety, set up the Windscale Inquiry in the mid-1970s, and there were later public inquiries concerning Sizewell and Hinkley Point.

Concorde

Concorde started in the Ministry of Supply, whose Permanent Secretary chaired the meeting that set up the Supersonic Transport Aircraft Committee (STAC); and whose minister, Aubrey Jones, suggested to the French in 1959 that they jointly develop Concorde with the British. Later it came under the Minister of Aviation, until transferring in 1966 to the Ministry of Technology. Following Labour's narrow election victory in February 1974, the DTI split into two. Tony Benn was in charge of Industry and looked after Concorde; while Peter Shore was in charge of Trade and oversaw British Airways (BA).

The Channel Tunnel

The Channel Tunnel and British Rail were the responsibility of many ministers of transport. As with Concorde, the Foreign Office must have worried from time to time about relations with the French. The Department of the Environment played an important part in choosing the route for the Channel Tunnel high-speed Rail Link (CTRL) to London. Even after the railways had been privatised, the Department of Transport continued in effective charge as the subsidies grew ever larger.

The Millennium Dome

The Dome came under many departments in its brief life: the government Shareholder at various times was the Chancellor of the Duchy of Lancaster (February–May 1997); the Secretary of State for National Heritage (May 1997); the Minister without Portfolio (June 1997–December 1998); the Secretary of State for Culture, Media and Sport (December 1998–January 1999); and the Minister of State at the Cabinet Office (from January 1999). This many homes in four years must be something of a record, though Chris Smith's two stints were very short: Roger Freeman, Peter Mandelson and finally Lord Falconer were the three main people in this role.

The chairmen of the Millennium Commission were Virginia Bottomley and Chris Smith, Secretaries of State for National Heritage (later renamed Culture, Media and Sport). In 2000 the sponsoring departments of the New Millennium Experience Company (NMEC) and English Heritage agreed to split the Dome's ultimate proceeds between them. The latter, the Department of the Environment, was concerned throughout with regenerating the Greenwich peninsula. As late as 2006, Deputy Prime Minister John Prescott still appeared to be involved with the possible use of the Dome as a super-casino.

How governments pay

The 'normal' way for governments to pay for a quasi-commercial project is through the annual budgets of the sponsoring department. But in practice the approach sometimes varies, which can make it extremely difficult to find out exactly how much a project *has* cost taxpayers. Given the pervasive emphasis on secrecy, perhaps that is not surprising.

Government accounting traditionally emphasised two things: proper authorisation by Parliament and controls against fraud. The commercial concept of 'a true and fair view', if not exactly alien, was not a top priority. Partly as a result government accounting has never been reliable. To give just one historical example: when the Post Office's accounts (then including telephones) were first audited by independent professional accountants, there were *two full pages* of 'qualifications'; even though the government's auditor-general had previously felt able to give an unqualified report.

R.101 airship

From year to year the Ministry of Aviation financed the Royal Airship Establishment at Cardington, researching into and building the R.101. The same ministry also financed the 'fixed-price' contract with the Airship Guarantee Company Limited, the Vickers subsidiary building the R.100, though the final cost was closer to £500,000 than the 'fixed' amount of the £350,000 contract. Also the ministry paid for related aspects of the airship work: the mooring masts (£160,000) and the Karachi base and shed (£120,000).

The groundnut scheme

The Ministry of Food financed the groundnut scheme, via the Overseas Food Corporation (OFC) (which had at first been going to finance a project in Queensland too). The OFC's £50 million capital was partly used to repay the United Africa Company, the Unilever subsidiary, their costs for running the project during the first year. The groundnut scheme had been planned to cost 'only' about £25 million; but when after about three years it had used up the whole of the OFC's £50 million, the government refused to reinforce failure by throwing more good money after bad. None of the other projects 'ran out of money' in quite the same way.

Nuclear power

It proved very difficult to work out what the costs of civil nuclear power amounted to, and if the AEA knew it was not saying. Henderson made some informed guesses, partly based on details in the SSEB's accounts. But the CEGB's accounts obscured the details, no doubt on purpose, by combining fossil fuels and nuclear energy. The AEA's own accounts needed to be (and mostly could be) split between military and civil. Only on privatisation were the real costs revealed, some of them (decommissioning) still far in the future.

Concorde

Because of the 50/50 arrangement with the French government, there must have been detailed accounts for Concorde all along. But until Tony Benn revealed them in 1974, the two governments kept the costs secret.[4] As noted earlier, the sponsoring department varied from time to time; and this may have made publishing the figures more difficult, even if the government had wanted to do so. BA's £160 million 'public dividend capital', used to purchase five Concordes in 1972, was written off in 1979.

Channel Tunnel

Eurotunnel was responsible for financing the design and building of the Channel Tunnel; but the British and French governments did provide important financial 'support' by extending the 55-year concession period, first by 10 years and then by a further 34 years. This probably never showed up anywhere as a 'cost'. They must also have spent some money on the Inter-Governmental Commission (IGC) and the Safety Authority. The British government financed probably more than half of the Channel Tunnel Rail Link to London (CTRL), in a number of different ways: by the Department of Transport subsidising British Rail and its privatised successors; by transferring land and other assets to London & Continental Railways (LCR), the consortium building the CTRL; probably by environmental spending; and by guaranteeing loans (to such an extent that the Office for National Statistics (ONS) said all LCR's debt should count as public sector debt).

Millennium Dome

The Department of the Environment, via English Partnerships, financed the purchase from British Gas of 294 acres on

---

4   Partly for military reasons, Feldman suggested (op. cit., pp. 97, 127, 139).

the Greenwich peninsula (of which the Millennium Exhibition used 130 acres); and paid for its regeneration. Most of the Dome expenditure came from grants via the Millennium Commission out of National Lottery funds, though there was some offsetting income (much less than expected) from sponsors and visitors.

Apart from the Channel Tunnel itself (which was Eurotunnel's problem), the government's attitude to overspending on all six projects (including CTRL) seemed to be that ultimately there was 'no alternative' to keeping the projects going. The OFC's initial £50 million capital proved a convenient excuse to abandon the groundnut scheme after three years of evident failure. The first Channel Tunnel project *was* cancelled on cost grounds in 1975. There was talk of cancelling Concorde on cost grounds and the Dome (for other reasons too), but in the end both projects survived. Nuclear power seemed immune to budget pressures throughout, until privatisation ended new investment.

Party politics

As a rule governments of both main parties share many features in common, so a change of government may make little difference. Also senior civil servants in the various ministries may provide continuity; although Alf Robens complained[5] that Ministry of Power civil servants were 'birds of passage', who were unable to challenge the AEA's nuclear energy figures. Moreover politicians of different parties often agree with their 'opponents'.

As long ago as 1894 Sir William Harcourt declared: 'We're all

5   Roger Williams, *The Nuclear Power Decisions, British Policies 1953–78*, Croom Helm, 1980, p. 158.

Socialists now.' And Halevy suggested in the 1930s: 'If you take a composite photograph of Lord Eustace Percy, Sir Oswald Mosley and Sir Stafford Cripps, … you would find them all agreeing to say: "We are living in economic chaos and we cannot get out of it except under some kind of dictatorial leadership."' Hayek, quoting this comment in 1944, added: 'The number of influential public men whose inclusion would not materially alter the features of the "composite photograph" has since grown considerably.'[6]

It may not seem surprising if the two main parties both edge towards the centre ground, though it is not what theory predicts[7] where (as in the UK) there are more than two parties. There appears today to be little difference in principle between Conservative and Labour policies on most subjects: defence, economic policy, the European Union, foreign policy, law and order, Northern Ireland, transport and the welfare state. About the only topic on which there might nowadays (for electoral reasons) be a difference is Scotland. So the two parties might well also adopt a similar attitude towards government projects.

There *were* sometimes party differences. For example, the Conservative government in 1923 was keener on private enterprise airships; though the Labour cabinet rejected Lord Thomson's proposal for a single government airship and instead decided on a competition between private and state enterprise. And it seems possible that a post-war Conservative government might have been less sanguine than Labour about the Wakefield Report's over-ambitious proposal for a mechanised groundnut scheme in a backward colony in East Africa.

---

6 F. A. Hayek, *The Road to Serfdom*, Routledge & Kegan Paul, London, 1944, p. 50 (dedicated 'To The Socialists Of All Parties').

7 See Gordon Tullock, *The Vote Motive*, rev. edn, IEA, London, 2006, pp. 57–8.

A Conservative government might have been keener than Labour on Common Market entry in the early 1960s, hence less inclined to risk upsetting the French by cancelling Concorde. Yet Macmillan could have cancelled Concorde *after* de Gaulle's first rejection in January 1963; and the subsequent Douglas-Home government did consider doing so. Mrs Thatcher insisted that private enterprise should finance and build any Channel Tunnel: a Labour government, which cancelled an earlier Channel Tunnel project on cost grounds, might have adopted it as a *government* project. Post-Thatcher, at least **£3,000 million** of 'public' money probably went into the Channel Tunnel Rail Link.

The strength of the 'nuclear establishment' prevented nuclear energy problems becoming party political. And there is little reason to attribute the Dome's shortcomings more to the 1997 Labour government than to the Conservative government between 1995 and 1997. Michael Heseltine played a large part in starting the Dome project and keeping it going. Moreover, it was the Conservatives who appointed as NMEC's chief executive a civil servant with no experience of running a visitor attraction; and whose Millennium Commission predicted a *minimum* of 15 million visitors.

Prime ministers seem not to have played a major part in the first two projects – the R.101 airship and the groundnut scheme. But the three next projects were all large enough to demand the prime minister's attention. Churchill's support must have been essential to begin the first civil nuclear power programme, and Macmillan's to *triple* its scale after Suez. We know Macmillan was important in approving the Concorde project.[8] Wilson seems to have been rather passive in the first Channel Tunnel project,

8   See Annabel May, 'Concorde – bird of harmony or political albatross?', *International Organization*, 33(4), Autumn 1979, p. 494.

but Thatcher's somewhat surprising keenness was crucial to the second.

Two *deputy* prime ministers, unusually, seem to have been important to the Millennium Dome project. Michael Heseltine was a robust supporter from start to finish, partly on environmental grounds, remaining a commissioner throughout; and John Prescott's backing may have been critical when the new Labour government was thinking about cancelling the Dome after the 1997 election. Apparently he told Blair: 'If we can't make this work, we're not much of a government.'[9]

Abandonment

The balance between expected future costs and benefits may shift over time until a project in progress no longer seems worthwhile. But it may not be obvious when this point has arrived; and changing one's mind may be politically embarrassing. If major projects span more than one parliament, the governing party may change during their lives. So a new incoming government might get a chance to review an existing enterprise, without much feeling of 'commitment'. Unless it is already too late, such a government may feel more able to cancel a project than a previous government which started it.

The R.101 airship project was contentious. Ramsay MacDonald's government changed the previous Baldwin government's decision to acquire six Vickers airships into a 'competition' between the Vickers R.100 and the government's R.101. The subsequent Conservative government did not reverse that decision,

---

9   Alastair Irvine, *The Battle for the Millennium Dome*, Irvine News Agency, 1999, p. 64.

though it could surely have considered doing so, returning to power less than six months later. After the R.101 crashed in October 1930, the Labour government abandoned the whole airship programme, including the R.100.

The groundnut scheme was the only project that a government of a different party had little or no chance to cancel. Stafford Cripps, the Labour Chancellor of the Exchequer, refused to invest any more money in 1949 after the OFC's £50 million capital was all gone. Then, after the February 1950 general election, a new Labour Minister of Food virtually scrapped the project after several years of failure; though it limped on for a few more years on a very much smaller scale.

It was hardly possible to 'cancel' the nuclear power stations; though after trebling the Churchill government's first programme in 1957, the Conservative government under Macmillan later somewhat reduced and delayed it. A new Labour government under Wilson need not have started the second nuclear programme in the mid-1960s either on the scale it chose or with British reactors; and privatisation at the end of the 1980s speedily and unexpectedly ended the Conservatives' much smaller third 'programme'.

Each of the three later projects spanned at least one change of governing party; and in each case the incoming government gave serious thought to cancellation. But government projects need not always involve 'party politics'. Concorde, the Channel Tunnel and the Millennium Dome (like nuclear power stations) were not really matters of *party* dispute.

The incoming Wilson government did attempt to cancel Concorde in January 1965, before promptly 'uncancelling' it when the French objected. The Heath government also considered cancelling Concorde some six years later, but decided not to do so – even though the Central Policy Review Staff was to call it 'a commercial disaster'.

The Douglas-Home government started the first post-war Channel Tunnel project in 1964. It survived two changes of government until the second Wilson government finally cancelled it in early 1975, after tunnelling had started. By then the UK had entered the European Common Market. Mrs Thatcher launched the second Tunnel project in 1985, and the Tunnel itself opened in 1994 during John Major's Conservative government. But the high-speed rail link to London was still not open when Blair left office thirteen years later.

When the private sector refused to finance the Millennium Dome in 1996 the Conservative government under Major might have considered dropping it. Instead it seems to have quickly decided to convert it into a government project. The incoming Labour government did consider cancelling the Dome in 1997, but support from Blair and Prescott (and probably Heseltine) carried the day. In 2007 Gordon Brown admitted this had been 'a mistake'. Once the Dome was open, nearly all the costs had already been incurred, hence closing it during 2000 never seemed economically attractive.

Conservative governments started six projects (all but the groundnut scheme) and chose to cancel none; though privatisation in 1989 put an end to new nuclear power stations, at least for a time. Labour governments decided to cancel four of the seven projects (counting two Channel Tunnel projects), only one of which they started, and thought about cancelling a fifth. It is tempting to suggest that Conservative governments tend to start large disastrous quasi-commercial projects and that Labour governments often try to cancel them; but the sample is really too small for any such conclusion.

National prestige

The government hoped all six projects would increase national 'prestige',[10] but only the two Anglo-French projects, Concorde and the Channel Tunnel, seem likely to have achieved this aim. While the English think the French are obsessed with national prestige, a number of post-war statesmen have boasted about Britain 'punching above her weight'. Aiming to increase national prestige might explain why governments take on projects that the private sector rejects. In practice it is hard to put a money value on 'prestige', and taxpayers may not feel it compensates them for large financial losses.

The R.101 team at Cardington felt they were working on a project of national importance, but it ended in a disastrous crash. The Permanent Secretary at the Ministry of Food refused to contemplate ending the groundnut scheme, because it involved British prestige; but the outcome could scarcely have been worse. Developing civil nuclear power, according to Gowing, was a matter of national prestige – 'at any cost', as it turned out. Concorde was clearly a prestige project, though Henderson attached little importance to it;[11] and not a single independent airline chose to buy the aircraft. Speaking about Concorde, Jo Grimond said: 'Whenever I hear the word "prestige", my heart sinks.'[12] The Channel Tunnel,

---

10   The word derives from a Latin word meaning 'trick', 'deception' or 'illusion'.

11   P. D. Henderson, 'Two British errors: their probable size and some possible lessons', *Oxford Economic Papers*, 1977, pp. 178–80.

12   House of Commons, 4 November 1964.

too, involved national prestige, even though private enterprise was building, financing and operating it. So did the CTRL, which took a further thirteen years to complete, and which in the end the government largely financed. And the Millennium Commission cited the 'reputation of the UK' to justify grants to the Dome that the accounting officer advised against.

Aiming to increase national prestige might explain why governments choose to take on projects that the private sector rejects. But in practice it is extremely hard to measure any change in 'prestige', or to put a money value on it. Even if taxpayers do not believe an increase in national prestige sufficiently compensates them for losses on government projects, they cannot do much about it. Global investors seeking financial returns are also unlikely to regard increasing *national* prestige as a worthwhile objective for the companies they own shares in.

Who is doing the valuing? It might be the 'international community', a nation's population as a whole, or just its politicians. The latter might explain governments being prepared to risk taxpayers' money to boost 'national prestige' which the taxpayers themselves scarcely value. *Relative* national prestige may be a zero-sum game,[13] where one nation gains what another loses. A major reason why the British were so delighted at 'winning' the 2012 Olympic Games (before the bills started to pour in) was that the 'victory' was at the expense of our age-old rivals, the French!

Secrecy

Secrecy was to some extent a factor in all the projects. Nevil Shute

---

[13]   A striking contrast to the market economy, in which both parties to a voluntary market transaction normally expect to gain from it.

said the Vickers team working on the R.100 airship knew what was going on with the government's R.101 only from what they read in the newspapers, and even Masefield[14] said 'the Air Ministry had played its cards close to its chest'. Shute and Masefield disagree[15] about who refused to talk to whom. Alan Wood, its public relations officer, said they ran the groundnut scheme as if it were a military operation, where 'loose talk would cost lives'. The AEA was extremely secretive about the development of civil nuclear technology and about its costs; and the Powell Committee's 1962 discussions about the economics of nuclear and conventional power were never published.

Only in 1974 did Tony Benn reveal what Concorde was costing – more than a decade after the project began in earnest. Without his insistence, financial obscurity might well have continued. There were complaints that safety aspects of the Channel Tunnel were being concealed behind a 'stone wall of secrecy': though Eurotunnel's status as a public company guaranteed a fair amount of transparency. The contents of the Millennium Dome were a mystery until just before it opened, which made advance marketing a nightmare; and the select committee said getting facts was like drawing teeth.

In many military projects, governments can – and arguably should – maintain almost complete financial secrecy. But 'quasi-commercial' government projects ought to be transparent, otherwise public comment and criticism are stifled. Indeed, a key argument for requiring stewardship accounting in business is to

---

14   Sir Peter Masefield, *To Ride the Storm: The Story of the Airship R.101*, William Kimber, London, 1982, p. 58.

15   See Nevil Shute, *Slide Rule*, Heinemann, London, 1954, p. 58, and Masefield, op. cit., p. 164.

affect the attitude of managers *in advance*.[16] The fact is, however, that British governments often seem to find it hard to 'come clean' about the financial aspects of projects. They prefer to be unaccountable, which is not an ultimate option for public companies.

The spiralling cost of the groundnut scheme was no secret, though the minister in charge tried to pretend that the revenues would be higher too. Tony Benn – a fervent advocate of 'open government' – revealed Concorde's costs after years of secrecy; but even he was unable to make much progress in revealing the true costs of nuclear power. This may simply have been because nobody knew what they were, or because those who did lied. And the monopoly providers of retail energy may have had insufficient incentive to care, since they expected to be able to pass the costs on to captive consumers.

It is extremely hard to see how much governments have spent on the Channel Tunnel Rail Link: there has been a curious mixture of direct Private Finance Initiative (PFI) grants, subsidies to British Rail and its successors, transfers of public assets and various guarantees. In addition, governments twice extended the 55-year concession period for the 'privately financed' Tunnel itself, first by ten years, then by a further 34 years: governments well understand that if you use a high enough discount rate, the apparent 'present value' of such giveaways can be made to seem negligible, if indeed they are included at all as part of the 'cost' to government. This was a way of transferring wealth to Eurotunnel without a – forbidden – cash subsidy.

Improving the environment was a reason for extra government spending on both the CTRL and the Dome. This, as well as

---

16   See D. R. Myddelton, *Unshackling Accountants*, IEA, London, 2004, pp. 28–30 and 41–2.

national prestige, is also likely to be an excuse for overspending on the 2012 Olympic Games. The Dome involved National Lottery money, and the government's pretence that it had nothing to do with them convinced nobody. £1,500 million, more than half the initial Olympic budget, came from National Lottery funds. Then, in March 2007 (in a much increased total budget of £9,325 million), a further £675 million was commandeered, making £2,175 million in all – so far. Thus it seems clear that we can regard disbursements from National Lottery funds as government spending.

Acronyms

AEA	Atomic Energy Authority
BA	British Airways
CEGB	Central Electricity Generating Board
CTRL	Channel Tunnel Rail Link
DTI	Department of Trade and Industry
IGC	Inter-Governmental Commission
LCR	London & Continental Railway
NMEC	New Millennium Experience Company
OFC	Overseas Food Corporation
ONS	Office of National Statistics
PFI	Private Finance Initiative
SSEB	South of Scotland Electricity Board
STAC	Supersonic Transport Aircraft Committee

9 COSTS AND BENEFITS

Cost and time overruns

Each of the projects failed by most of the four criteria. The R.101 airship and the groundnut scheme failed to deliver the end-product. In the three projects where customers were directly relevant, demand in each case was less than half the forecast level. All six projects cost the government far more than expected, even ignoring interest on capital. Only on the airship programme was the cost overrun much less than 100 per cent. And all except the Dome took much longer to complete than planned (treating the high-speed rail link to London as part of the Channel Tunnel 'project').

Three projects (Concorde, the Channel Tunnel and the Millennium Dome) did succeed in producing the end-product. (Nuclear power only partly succeeded, the stations' capacity being much less than planned.) Overall, therefore, as the Summary Table shows, there was some success in producing the end-product, very little in meeting time objectives, and failure on the other two measures.

The government-designed R.101 airship crashed on its maiden flight to India, killing all but six of the 54 people on board. The whole programme (including the Vickers R.100, which succeeded in flying to Canada and back) was then abandoned: it cost **£100**

Table 12 Summary of project out-turns

	R.101	Groundnuts	Nuclear power		Concorde	Channel Tunnel		Dome
			1: Magnox	2: AGR		Tunnel	CTRL	
End-product	No	No	Yes	Yes	Yes	Yes	Nearly	Yes
Costs (2007 £m)					(total)	(Eurotunnel)	(to gov't)	(to gov't)
Plan	60	600	17,000	14,500	2,400	5,000	0	500
Actual	100	1,150	n/a	n/a	9,600	9,350	3,000	1,000
Overrun: £m	40	550	10,800+	21,200	7,200	4,350	3,000	500
Overrun: %	67	92	63+	146	300	87		100
Time (years)								
Plan	2.7	6.0	4.1	6	6.2	7.0	7	3.0
Actual	6.4	5.0	7.8	12+	13.0	8.0	22	3.0
Overrun: years	3.7	n/a	3.7	6+	6.8	1.0	15	0
Overrun: %	137	n/a	90	100+	110	14	214	0
Demand/capacity	Passengers	'000 tonnes (output p.a.)	MW	MW	Sales	Passengers (in 2003)		Visitors
Plan	100	600	5,500	10,500	100–250	39.5 m	n/a	12.0m
Actual	25	virtually nil	3,800	7,300	9	14.7 m	n/a	5.5m
Shortfall: numbers	75	nearly 600	1,700	3,200	91+	24.8 m	n/a	6.5m
Shortfall: %	75	nearly 100	31	30	91+	63	n/a	54

million instead of **£60 million**. This 67 per cent overrun was due mainly to the project taking more than twice as long as planned.

In order to reduce Britain's food bill by **£250 million** a year, the groundnut scheme aimed to clear 3.2 million acres in East Africa and grow 600,000 tonnes of groundnuts a year. The project cost about **£1,150 million** instead of **£600 million**, an overrun of 92 per cent; and the scheme cleared only about 100,000 acres. So there was virtually no end-product and there were no savings.

Nuclear power stations greatly overran on both cost and time, and under-provided output capacity by about one third. They produced electricity costing at least 25 per cent more than energy produced using fossil fuel power. Quantifying the total cost overruns is not easy: my estimate is *at least* **£32,000 million**, or more than 100 per cent.

Concorde's costs, kept secret for years, totalled **£9,600 million**, an overrun of 300 per cent in real terms. The aircraft took thirteen years to design and build, twice as long as planned, and no independent airline chose to buy it.

The Channel Tunnel, a privately financed project, cost **£9,350 million**, an overrun of 87 per cent. The equity shareholders and the bank lenders bore most of this cost, the contractors some of it. The Tunnel took one year longer than the planned seven years to build (not a big delay for a large transport project). The high-speed rail link to London cost about **£5,750 million** (of which at least **£3,000 million** was government money); and it was thirteen years 'late', which may help explain why customer demand fell so far short of forecast.

The Dome's overall cost estimates were somewhat too low; and the gross overspend, even excluding a large contingency allowance (which turned out not to be enough), was only about 18 per cent.

But combined with failure to attract enough visitors, this doubled the government's residual contribution (including regeneration and lottery funds) from **£500 million** to **£1,000 million**.

For the two Anglo-French projects one needs care in assessing the net costs to British taxpayers. For Concorde the two governments each had to bear roughly half the total costs; but for the Channel Tunnel things are not so simple. Nearly all the costs of designing and constructing the 1985 Tunnel were borne by Eurotunnel, not by the governments. But the British government did bear a substantial part of the costs of building the high-speed rail link to London; though the arrangements were so complex and obscure that it is hard to be precise.

In computing the total costs of projects I have generally excluded interest on the amounts expended (as is usual when reporting such costs). So in a sense the costs and the overruns are understated. There are two exceptions. First, Henderson's estimates[1] of the excess cost of Advanced Gas-cooled Reactor (AGR) nuclear power stations over their best rival, the American Light Water Reactors (LWRs), do include interest. I have taken these as one element in the total 'losses'. Second, Eurotunnel's total costs (and the resulting losses) include interest on the amounts borrowed, though the cost of constructing the Tunnel itself does not (this does not affect the cost to government of the Channel Tunnel Rail Link [CTRL]).

It is not easy to calculate how much difference including interest would make to the net cost of each project, though the longer the project, the more the difference. Adding simple (not compound) interest at 4 per cent a year I reckon would add about

---

1   For details see P. D. Henderson, 'Two British errors: their probable size and some possible lessons', *Oxford Economic Papers*, July 1977, pp. 159–205.

one third to the costs of the three large projects – nuclear power, Concorde and the CTRL. For the R.101 airship and the Millennium Dome, the increase would be about one tenth; and for the groundnut scheme only about one twentieth.

Alternative view of costs

Even allowing for inflation may result in somewhat misleading cost comparisons, given the far higher real level of national income at the end of the twentieth century than at the beginning.[2] Real growth of, say, 2 per cent a year for 50 years would nearly *triple* national income. In other words, projects may have been 'more affordable' towards the end of the period than at the beginning – a given real cost would have been a much higher proportion of national income in 1923 than in 2007.

I have tried to allow for this by estimating the national income per head (in current money terms) at the mid-point of each project; and seeing how many thousand man-years of income the total cost to government amounted to in each case. There must be a big margin of error, so the numbers are rounded to avoid spurious accuracy. The results are shown in Table 13.

Perhaps the most striking change is that, in terms of man-years of income, a recent project, the Dome, turns out to be only three times more costly than the earliest, the R.101 airship programme, rather than ten times more costly in 'real' terms. Also, the post-war groundnut scheme is about 10 per cent *more* expensive than the estimated cost to government of the recent CTRL, rather than just over one third as expensive.

---

2   Christian Wignall suggested this point.

Table 13 **The 'real' costs of the six projects: alternative approach**

Project	Middle year	Total money cost, £m	National income per head*, £	Man-years of income, '000s	Real cost, 2007 £m
R.101 airship	1927	2.4	94	25	100
Millennium Dome	1999	858	11,800	75	1,000
CTRL	2003	3,000	14,000	215	3,000
Groundnut scheme	1948	46	190	240	1,150
Concorde	1974	1,270	1,200	1,050	9,600
Nuclear power	1987	16,000	7,000	2,300	32,000

* Calculated for the middle year.

Cost overruns in general

All three very large projects (nuclear power, Concorde and the Channel Tunnel) suffered from unrealistic initial cost estimates. These were largely due to underestimating or ignoring each of the following three main generic causes of cost overruns:[3]

- the high risks of technological innovation;
- changes in project specifications and designs;
- evolving safety and environmental demands.

A 1988 Rand Corporation study[4] of 52 large civil infrastructure projects reported an average cost overrun of 88 per cent and an average time delay of 17 per cent. Both those averages almost exactly match the Channel Tunnel's results. A more

---

3 Summarised from Bent Flyvbjerg, Nils Bruzelius and Werner Rothengatter, *Megaprojects and Risk: An Anatomy of Ambition*, Cambridge University Press, 2003.

4 Quoted in Terry Gourvish, *The Official History of Britain and the Channel Tunnel*, Routledge, London, 2006, p. 366.

recent study[5] of 258 transport projects in twenty countries found that:

- nine out of ten projects underestimated costs;
- actual costs averaged 28 per cent higher than estimates (rail 45 per cent; tunnels and bridges 34 per cent; and roads 20 per cent);
- cost overruns have not decreased over the past 70 years.

The conclusion was that cost overruns are best explained, not by error, but by 'strategic misrepresentation' – *lying* – in order to get projects started. This applied to non-transport projects too. Strong incentives and weak disincentives seem to have taught project promoters that it *pays* to deliberately underestimate costs. Hence cost estimates used in public debates and decision-making are 'systematically and significantly deceptive'.

With respect to costs, competent responsible business managers should:

- forecast prudently, not optimistically, with a range of possible outcomes;
- include realistic contingency allowances;
- not publicly announce 'lowest possible' cost estimates;
- frequently update their own estimates as new information becomes available;
- try to give subcontractors appropriate incentives.

---

5 Bent Flyvbjerg, Mette K. Holm and Soren L. Buhl, 'Underestimating costs in public works projects: error or lie?', *Journal of American Planning Association*, 68(3), Summer 2002, pp. 279–95.

But few of the projects followed any of these requirements.

If politicians insist on going ahead 'at all costs', taxpayers should not be surprised at large cost overruns. It is mainly technical problems which cause 'unexpected' delays: though everyone knew that nuclear power stations and Concorde involved huge scientific and engineering challenges. 'Cost-plus' contracts may not represent much incentive to keep prices down but there is a limit to how much risk subcontractors will accept. It seems the Treasury does very sensibly now include contingency allowances in all major projects,[6] to correct the 'tendency for project appraisers to be overly optimistic'; though (as with the Dome) they may still not be large enough.

Owing to rapid post-war inflation between 1965 and 1980, project costs tended to increase much faster *in current money terms* than in 'real' terms. Project opponents – and even academics[7] – were sometimes unfair in failing to recognise this. Thirty years elapsed between the start of the first Channel Tunnel project in 1964 and the opening of the Tunnel in 1994. During that period, the pound lost no less than *90 per cent* of its purchasing power. Had physical measurements shrunk to the same extent, the Tunnel would have been only about three miles long!

Scope

With respect to benefits, competent business managers should:

---

6   *Financial Times*, 24 November 2006.

7   For example, Flyvbjerg et. al., *Megaprojects*, op. cit., p. 19, refer to a Concorde cost over-run of 1,100 per cent without recognising that the Retail Prices Index *trebled* between 1962 and 1976.

- spell out the project's main purpose precisely;
- where possible quantify the hoped-for benefits;
- forecast realistically the range of likely customer demand;
- not publicly announce 'highest possible' market estimates;
- frequently update their own estimates.

Again, few of the projects met any of the above requirements.

In none of the projects was the scope easy to define precisely.

- Was the scope of the R.101 'project' the successful construction of the government airship, in which case it failed? Or was it part of the joint programme with the private enterprise R.100, which was a partial success?
- Was the groundnut scheme the grandiose plan for 107 units of 30,000 acres each including Northern Rhodesia and Kenya? Or was it confined to the three large areas in Tanganyika where planting actually began?
- Did the nuclear power project comprise only the two main nuclear power station programmes? Or did it also include work on the very expensive but abortive Fast Breeder Reactor?
- Was the Concorde project only the long-haul version of the supersonic transport (SST)? Or did it at first also encompass the medium-range version the French preferred?
- Was the Channel Tunnel project the tunnel under the sea between Folkestone and Calais? Or should that be regarded (as in this book) as merely a key part of the project to build a high-speed railway between London and Paris?
- Was the Dome simply the building at Greenwich, and its contents? Or was it really an appendage of regenerating the

Greenwich peninsula (which did not require building a Dome on it)?

Scale

Having a promising idea for a large new project is a good start. But one always needs to see whether one can make it better. This may involve trying to improve the likely returns, either by increasing the benefits or by reducing the costs (or both); or by reducing the chances (risks) of things going wrong. The military say time spent on reconnaissance is seldom wasted. That is good advice for large commercial projects too.

The only project on which the government of the day seems to have decided to go ahead after hardly any reflection was the groundnut scheme. It may not be a coincidence that this was the only one that produced virtually no benefit. In all the other cases, governments seem to have agonised – one might almost say shilly-shallied – for *years* before making a decision. These were often not easy choices to make.

Scale was unimportant for two of the large projects. Market considerations meant the long-range transatlantic SST was the only realistic option for Concorde (though initially the French preferred a medium-range version). And the twin-bore rail tunnel was the cheapest version for the Channel Tunnel.

Evidently the Wakefield Report's proposal for the groundnut scheme in East Africa was on a colossal scale (3.2 million acres); though the report itself actually envisaged that 'given the will this target figure could be vastly exceeded [*sic*] in course of time'. In practice, given the nous, the original 3.2-million-acre target could have been very substantially *reduced*.

There was little need to *triple* the first nuclear power station programme (to up to 6GW), which seems to have been the Macmillan government's panic reaction to Suez. Nor need the second programme have been as large as 8GW (subsequently increased to a target of 10.5GW). Both ambitious programmes assumed faster growth in consumer demand than was actually attained as well as costs that were much lower than those incurred.

Lord Thomson would have preferred to go ahead only with the R.101 airship (not the private enterprise R.100 too, in 'competition' with it); though the 'fixed' costs of mooring masts at Ismailia and Karachi would have remained. Finally the Millennium Exhibition could have been on a much smaller scale than the grandiose Dome project and need not have involved the costly regeneration of the Greenwich peninsula (nor the Jubilee Line Extension's double crossing of the Thames).

Customers

Three projects had direct customers: Concorde, the Channel Tunnel and the Millennium Dome. In each case estimates of demand turned out to be far too high. They were probably influenced by engineers inspired by a technical challenge, politicians aiming for national 'prestige', and promoters anxious to get 'their' project approved. All of these may have carried more weight than accountants worrying about profit or loss. The trouble is that if demand estimates are far too high, not only will the number of customers be lower than forecast, but also the average *selling price* may well be lower than forecast too. This, of course, then has a 'double whammy' effect on *sales revenue* received.

It seems striking how high forecasts of sales remained even after part of their margin of error ought to have become apparent. This was also true both of aggregate energy demand forecasts affecting the nuclear power programmes and of production estimates for the groundnut scheme. In contrast Miller says: 'The private enterprise regime of the mid-nineteenth century ensured that the extra costs of the perhaps inevitable appraisal optimism of the very large projects involving new technology were borne by the shareholders – and not taxpayers.'[8] As he points out: 'Investors are volunteers, taxpayers are conscripts.' (This point was clearly relevant for the Channel Tunnel.)

Forecasting demand for Concorde must have been much harder than for the Channel Tunnel or the Dome. The aircraft was aiming for international sales in an extremely competitive market for a unique high-ticket item. Guessing the likely sales level of any new product is never easy, especially ten or more years in advance. In fact it is not clear whether anyone ever took the Concorde 'estimates' seriously. In all three cases it looks very much as though the promoters came up with deliberately optimistic numbers to get the project accepted. The most absurd estimate was in the Millennium Commissioners' guidelines to bidding sites for the Dome, which envisaged a *minimum* of 15 million visitors.

Flyvbjerg et al. found[9] that 18 out of a sample of 27 rail projects *overestimated* traffic forecasts by more than two-thirds. So it was surprising for Colin Stannard, one-time managing director of Eurotunnel PLC, to assert that: 'Even the most professional traffic

---

8   Robert C. B. Miller, *railway.com*, Research Monograph 57, IEA, London, 2003, pp. 23–4.

9   Flyvbjerg et al., *Megaprojects*, op. cit., p. 26.

forecast is highly likely to be conservative.'[10] Actual Channel Tunnel passenger numbers for 2003 were 60 per cent below the 1987 forecast (an 'overestimate' of 150 per cent), and freight traffic was 35 per cent below forecast.[11]

Politicians without a commercial background often seem not to care much about the end-customer for their projects. They tend to concentrate (though not always very effectively) on the cost of the inputs rather than on the value of outputs: that is one reason why the state schooling and health monopolies have such dreadfully poor results. 'Investment' as such is not a 'good thing', as some statesmen pretend or imply: it is merely spending in the hope of a future benefit. What *is* a good thing in the market system is *profitable* investment, and what makes it so is the profit! That means getting back from satisfied customers *more* than the total cost (including interest on capital).

Once governments have published optimistic forecasts of customer demand for projects, they can find it politically very difficult to reduce them. But people seem to expect *costs* to go up – partly because persistent inflation over recent generations has made everyone aware that the value of money is not stable. So increasing cost estimates is perhaps less embarrassing than reducing demand estimates.

What did the projects achieve?

The R.101 airship project created a great deal of knowledge about the technology and economics of airship construction. Everyone

10   Colin J. Stannard, 'Managing a mega-project – the Channel Tunnel', *Long Range Planning*, 23(5), 1990, pp. 54–5.

11   Gourvish, op. cit., p. 370.

knew this was a high-risk project; but the R.100 airship (the private enterprise part of the project) managed to overcome the risks on its flight to Canada and back.

The groundnut scheme achieved very little, and at great expense. This project seems to be the only one of the six to have produced virtually no worthwhile benefits. Even some of the infrastructure in Tanganyika soon had to be abandoned.

The scientists and engineers overcame very difficult technical problems to enable nuclear power stations to provide 20 per cent of the country's energy for many years. And nuclear power brings environmental benefits compared with fossil fuels.

Concorde was a marvellous technical achievement, and a beautiful iconic aeroplane. It also satisfied many regular passengers for over 25 years. It probably did raise the prestige of both France and Britain in the USA, which spent heavily on its own abortive SST project.

The Channel Tunnel provided a transport link between England and France, which had been mooted for more than a hundred years. An essential part of the project eventually provided a high-speed railway between the Tunnel and London.

The Millennium Dome was the most popular attraction in the country in the year 2000 and most visitors enjoyed their experience. Moreover, it was linked with regeneration of the Greenwich peninsula – which, indeed, may have been the project's primary purpose.

Risks

There are two main business kinds of project risk: technical and commercial. The former relates to whether we can make the project work and the latter to whether we can sell it to customers. The R.101 airship never completely overcame its structural challenges, nor is it clear that there would have been a market. Nevil Shute asserted that senior men in the Air Ministry knew that 'abnormal and quite unjustifiable risks were being taken with R.101'.[12] But 'they failed to speak up against Lord Thomson because they were afraid ... the men in question put their jobs before their duty'.

All the other projects were risky too. If it had been possible to grow 600,000 tons of groundnuts a year, the Overseas Food Corporation (OFC) could surely have sold them on the world market, though at an uncertain price. Concorde solved huge engineering problems, at a huge cost; but there were no willing buyers for the aircraft. Technical troubles affected both nuclear power stations and the Channel Tunnel. In both cases the end-product was less competitive than was originally hoped. The same was true, on a smaller scale, of the Dome.

The main argument for involving governments in quasi-commercial projects seems to be that they may be able and willing to bear larger *risks* than commercial companies can tolerate. Government projects may also involve *political* risks; though only the R.101 airship and the groundnut scheme were matters of party dispute. Both the Anglo-French projects – Concorde and the (first) Channel Tunnel – arose when Britain was applying to join the Common Market. And both nuclear power and Concorde pitted British technology against US competition.

Making proper allowance for project risk and uncertainty is

---

12 Shute, op. cit., pp. 146–8. He went on to suggest that men with private means were more likely to express independent views, hence high inheritance taxes were very damaging to a high-quality civil service.

extremely difficult. With 'risk' you know the odds, as when playing roulette, but 'uncertainty' means you *don't* know the odds. Clearly each of the six projects was unique, hence not directly susceptible to frequency probability. Describing a suitable approach can give a false impression. For instance, in 1968 the Atomic Energy Authority (AEA) said of a nuclear development programme: it was 'only authorised if, over a credible range of assumptions, benefits exceed costs by a factor judged against the probability of success'.[13]

But these plausible-sounding words raise a number of difficult questions:

- Did *some* 'credible' assumptions lie *outside* the 'credible range of assumptions' actually used? If so, why exclude them?
- Can one measure all 'benefits' (including, for example, 'national prestige')? If not, how can one sensibly compare them with costs?
- Did anyone in 1968 really *know* all the 'costs' of nuclear power?
- At what rate of interest should estimates of future benefits and costs be discounted back to 'present value'?[14]
- How did the AEA define 'success' – in financial or in technical terms?
- How does one attempt to measure the 'probability of success'?

For uncertain projects you cannot tell in advance what the

---

13 Quoted in Roger Williams, *The Nuclear Power Decisions, British Policies 1953–78*, Croom Helm, 1980, p. 199, from the 1967/68 Annual Report, para. 191.

14 This was a critical assumption in the recent Stern Report on climate change.

odds are against success. Nor even *after* a 'successful' event can you be sure how close you came to disaster.[15] It is hardly surprising if very risky projects on the frontiers of known technology sometimes 'go wrong'. Whether, on balance, it was sensible to take the risks depends partly on the possible rewards of 'success'; partly on the costs; and partly on how well one has understood the major risks and whether one has taken suitable steps to mitigate or manage them.

For the six projects, what kind of risks were either unforeseen, or failed to occur?

- With the R.101 airship, the eventual emergence of aeroplanes that could carry hundreds of passengers thousands of miles in moderate comfort was not foreseen.
- Most of the things that could have gone wrong with the groundnut scheme did go wrong, except a collapse in the market price of groundnuts.
- The main risk to the nuclear power programmes – problems in getting the technology to work – did in fact transpire, while very extensive safety precautions succeeded in limiting serious accidents. Nobody seems to have expected either the huge problems – and costs – of decommissioning or the emergence of North Sea oil and gas as rival fossil fuels.
- With Concorde, unlike with both the Boeing SSTs, governments (British and French) maintained their support for the long-range version. Withdrawal at any time would have ended the project. But they did not fully predict the difficulties of selling the aircraft or the noise problems.

---

15   For example, the outcome of the Falklands War, like that of the Battle of Waterloo, was a very close-run thing.

- Perhaps the most serious risk for the Channel Tunnel was a bomb exploding in the Tunnel. This hasn't happened yet, though there has been a fire. There were three competitive risks that traffic forecasters did not fully anticipate: the survival of the ferries, the attraction of budget airlines and the very long delay in completing the high-speed rail link from the Tunnel to London.
- Three essentials for the Millennium Dome project were time-related (see below): decontaminating the site, completing the Jubilee Line Extension before the Dome opened and getting the Dome's building and contents ready in time. Failure in any one of these would have been disastrous.

Time

Where a project sponsor is paying for people's time, the longer the project takes the more it is likely to cost. So time overruns and cost overruns tend to go together. But for several of the projects time was not regarded as very important, any more than money was.

Owing mainly to technical problems, the R.101 airship (like the R.100) took more than twice as long to design and construct as initially planned. So the demonstration flight to India began not in January 1927 but in October 1930. But this delay seemed to matter only when it threatened Lord Thomson's insistence on returning from India in time for the Imperial Conference in mid-October. Then time became so critical that essential safety precautions were ignored.

It hardly mattered whether the groundnut scheme got under way in 1947 or 1949, and there was always plenty of time for a pilot scheme first. But the Minister of Food, John Strachey, seemed to believe that time was of the essence: hence the decision to go ahead only six weeks after receiving the Wakefield Report. In this (rare) case there turned out to be a *financial* constraint. Once the OFC's £50 million capital had run out, the '£25 million' project was over.

Time was clearly a factor for both nuclear power programmes. The expected production period was many years, with a useful reactor life of fifteen to twenty years or more. But there was no special hurry and, owing to technical and labour problems, there were long delays before the reactors were ready. This mattered less than it might have done, since consumer demand grew more slowly than forecast. Some aspects of decommissioning involved very long time periods indeed.

At one stage the Anglo-French Concorde had a three- to four-year advantage over the rival US SST. But when the Boeing project was finally cancelled in 1971, nearly all the time pressure was relieved. So the large production time overrun due mainly to technical problems had little commercial consequence. The price of Concorde was not critical to sales, since owing to the running costs, independent airline customers were not interested. PanAm said it would not want the aircraft even if it were *given* away.[16]

Building the Channel Tunnel was a private enterprise. Because it was largely financed by borrowed money, time was critical, and the contractors faced severe penalties for delay. Even so, the one-year time overrun (on a seven-year project) was almost fatal to Eurotunnel, both because of interest on the loans and because of the delay to revenues. The government part of the project was the high-speed rail link to London (CTRL). This proved to be a

16 Elliot J. Feldman, *Concorde and Dissent: Explaining high technology failures in Britain and France*, Cambridge University Press, 1985, p. 95.

much more leisurely affair, taking more than *thirteen* years until it was complete.

Time really was critical for the Millennium Dome, of course, with its overriding need to open not a single day later than 1 January 2000. Three separate time-sensitive aspects were decontaminating the land at Greenwich, completing the Jubilee Line extension (JLE) through North Greenwich, and designing and producing the Dome's contents. The first two were achieved in time (the JLE with not much to spare); but, owing perhaps partly to time pressure, the Dome's contents and infrastructure fell short of ideal. It was suggested that holding separate competitions for the site and for the exhibition operators may have cost up to a year.

Acronyms

AEA	Atomic Energy Authority
AGR	Advanced Gas-cooled Reactor
CTRL	Channel Tunnel Rail Link
GW	Gigawatts
JLE	Jubilee Line Extension
LWR	Light Water Reactor
OFC	Overseas Food Corporation
SST	Supersonic transport

10 CONCLUSIONS

Government versus private enterprise

Tocqueville says that in France before the Revolution: 'It never occurred to anyone that any large-scale enterprise could be put through successfully without the intervention of the State.'[1] That has rarely been so in England: indeed, for large parts of our history, quite the contrary. We have always been suspicious of grandiose state projects, and rather surprised if they *don't* end in abject failure. Jewkes asks rhetorically: 'Which is the best way of picking the winners, leaving it to governments or leaving it to private effort and the market?'[2] He also suggests that governments ought to concentrate on better fulfilling their primary tasks – defence, law and order, etc.

If governments encounter so many problems in tackling large quasi-commercial projects, why do they choose to get involved in the first place? 'Do nothing' is always an option, but it may not appeal to interventionist governments. Jewkes says 'companies, in close contact with realities, will not give [such projects] their support because the chances of profit seem too small, problematical or remote; but … the government, for one reason or another,

---

1   Alexis de Tocqueville, *The Ancien Regime and the French Revolution*, Fontana, London, 1966, p. 95.
2   John Jewkes, *Government and High Technology*, IEA, London, 1972, pp. 10, 24.

feels that it knows better. Private enterprise will not jeopardise the requisite shareholders' capital, but governments feel justified in risking the taxpayers' money'.[3]

That may be unfair. Sometimes project risks are so great that private enterprise companies simply cannot afford to undertake them. Only governments may be willing and able to bear such risks. Indeed, following Keynes,[4] one might argue that governments should take on such projects *only* when companies are *not* willing to do so. But then perhaps such projects may not be *worth* taking on.

Do governments measure the likely net 'returns' (or benefits) in much the same way as commercial entities? In fact the criteria for success are not always clear. Financial success – meaning accounting profits large enough to cover the cost of risky equity capital – may not be all that the politicians seek. Also they may not be so concerned with avoiding losses. Hence they may shrink from abandoning projects if it is politically embarrassing to do so. It is possible that governments *might* attach weight to 'benefits' that are of little concern to profit-seeking businesses, such as national prestige, but I doubt whether that is often important *ex ante*. The achievement of benefits such as national prestige may sometimes be used as an excuse when everyone can see that, from a commercial point of view, a project is 'going wrong'.

But governments may look at the *risks* differently. Ministers and civil servants sometimes seem not to realise or care about the scale of the risks they are taking – with other people's money. Everyone knew that Concorde and nuclear power involved large

3   Ibid., pp. 7–8.
4   J. M. Keynes, *The End of Laissez-Faire* (1926), *Collected Works*, vol. IX, Macmillan, London, 1972, p. 291.

scientific and engineering risks; but technical overconfidence seems to have been a factor in both the R.101 airship disaster and the groundnut scheme fiasco. And the Millennium Commission's early guideline of a *minimum* of 15 million visitors to the Dome suggests a serious failure to understand market risks.

There may be wisdom in Adam Smith's somewhat jaundiced view of governments attempting to manage mercantile projects:

> whether such a government as that of England; which, whatever may be its virtues, has never been famous for good economy; which, in time of peace, has generally conducted itself with the slothful and negligent profusion that is perhaps natural to monarchies; and in time of war has constantly acted with all the thoughtless extravagance that democracies are apt to fall into; could be safely trusted with the management of such a project [as running a bank], must at least be ... doubtful. ... Princes ... have frequently engaged in many other mercantile projects [other than the post office]. ... They have scarce ever succeeded.[5]

The six projects reviewed
R.101 airship

The 1923 Conservative government decided to go for six airships from Vickers. That would have avoided 'spreading the experts too thinly', and without costing much more in total on construction. Research and development costs for a *single* airship – rather than two very different ones – could have been spread over six Vickers airships; while the 'infrastructure' costs of mooring masts, etc., would have remained much the same. Instead of accepting this,

5   Adam Smith, *The Wealth of Nations*, 1776, Book V, ch. II, pt I.

Ramsay MacDonald's Labour government chose a 'competition' between private enterprise and government (R.100 versus R.101). At least that was better than Lord Thomson's proposal for *only* a government airship. The failure to put R.101C through proper flight trials resulted in taking far too much risk on her maiden flight to India. Such imprudence would have been unlikely with a commercial airship, lacking the intense political pressure.

The groundnut scheme

Unilever's United Africa Company (UAC) subsidiary felt unable to take on a project of anything like the scope the Wakefield Report envisaged. UAC's Frank Samuel thought only a government could undertake such a huge venture, but it was the risks as well as the size which ruled it out. The Labour government should have asked: do we really have a comparative advantage in growing groundnuts on a vast scale in an African colony? Why don't we just *buy* groundnuts (or other sources of fat) on the world market? Or would it be better to let private enterprise do even that? But such a market-oriented approach may have seemed out of the question: the post-war socialist euphoria proved very expensive.

Nuclear power

The post-war UK electricity supply industry was nationalised and the 'nuclear establishment' consisted entirely of government employees. So there was no chance of private British companies deciding to build one or more nuclear power stations, as several of their US counterparts did. Privatising the industry at that time would have been a start towards letting the market work. It would almost certainly have produced more accurate cost estimates, and probably better business decisions too. Private enterprise might have invested in nuclear power on a station-by-station basis, if it seemed likely to make a profit: though there was a huge amount of learning to gain by building more than one station (which the government largely let slip). In any event, private enterprise managers would surely have been much less casual about trying to discover the true costs, though no doubt this would still have been very difficult. The present Labour government has said[6] that any new nuclear power stations will have to be built by the private sector without state support – a revealing sign of how far opinions have changed.

Concorde

Private enterprise's obvious reluctance to take on such a huge and risky project meant Concorde had to be a government project or it would not have taken place. Sir James Hamilton pointed out how difficult it was to provide any financial discipline for contractors. Indeed, the project's size and risks were so large that the British decided it had to be a *two*-government project, with all the problems that caused. Had the two state airlines been privatised at the time, sales of Concorde might have been literally zero! On four separate occasions the British government considered cancelling the project, on grounds of cost.

---

6   DTI, *The Energy Challenge*, July 2006, esp. para. 5.96.

The Channel Tunnel

Was Mrs Thatcher right to insist that the (second) Channel Tunnel project could go ahead in the mid-1980s only if it was privately financed? Many private equity and loan investors lost most of their money in Eurotunnel, which probably 'justifies' her decision, from the taxpayers' point of view. And in this instance the government really does seem to have made a big effort not to interfere in building the Tunnel. But this was a 'government' project for two reasons: ownership of the Tunnel reverts to the British and French governments after 99 years (originally after 55 years), and the two governments (or, rather, their taxpayers) largely paid for the high-speed rail links between the Tunnel and London and Paris respectively.

The Millennium Dome

We know the government hoped that a private enterprise would volunteer to operate the Millennium Dome. Would it really have mattered if the government had abandoned the idea when no private enterprise proved willing to accept the risks? No important objective was at stake – unless the real purpose was to restore the Greenwich peninsula, with the Dome Exhibition merely an optional add-on. It was a Conservative government – under John Major – which took the New Millennium Experience Company (NMEC) into public ownership to operate the Dome. The new Labour government in 1997 urgently considered cancelling it, on grounds of cost. Perhaps they should have done so.

Thus market solutions might have meant no groundnut scheme, no Concorde and no Millennium Dome. There might have been fewer, if any, nuclear power stations; and possibly no Channel Tunnel if a privatised British Rail had been unwilling to invest in a high-speed link to London. But perhaps there *would* have been six Vickers (R.100-type) airships, less technically adventurous than the government-built R.101. Paying a finite subsidy to a private enterprise for a limited period would greatly have reduced the dangerous open-ended nature of a 'government project'.

If we had known …

Had the governments foreseen the outcomes, would they still have decided, first, to go ahead with and then not to cancel each of the projects?

The R.101 airship programme (together with the R.100) did achieve substantial progress. It may be, with hindsight, that it would have been better to maintain the original decision to contract with Vickers for six private enterprise airships. The 'competition' between government and private enterprise stretched national resources thinly. It also overlooked the government's poor record in building aircraft and meant that no independent group was able to check on the Royal Airship Works at Cardington.

The Attlee government would surely not have started the groundnut scheme if it had foreseen the outcome, or anything like it. It was about as complete a fiasco as you could ever find. A pilot scheme would have revealed many of the basic problems. Once started, even disastrously, political momentum made it difficult to stop the project, even though the sponsoring minister was not in the cabinet.

The nuclear power programmes turned out to be incredibly expensive. If the government had fully foreseen the costs, surely it would not have tripled the 'first' nuclear programme after Suez, given knowledge of the actual extent and timing of increased consumer demand. The government might still have decided to diversify sources of fuel away from coal and oil; but for the second programme it would have done better to buy US rather than further develop discredited 'British' technology.

Concorde would almost certainly not have been started if the government had predicted the failure to sell any aircraft – quite apart from the huge costs, which the Treasury (though not all ministers) probably did more or less anticipate. Thorneycroft, the Minister of Aviation, said: 'Looking back, I would say on the figures, I don't think I would have done it.' And John Davies, Secretary of State for Trade and Industry, said that if he had been chairman of a company, responsible to shareholders, he would have cancelled Concorde.[7]

Financial institutions and private investors would not have financed the Channel Tunnel if they had foreseen the low level of demand. Fund-raising was a near thing as it was. The Tunnel itself simply was not the 'fully commercial operation' that Thatcher and Ridley had demanded. Nor was the high-speed rail link to London, for which the government bore most of the cost: the Channel Tunnel Rail Link (CTRL) was extremely expensive and never really looked like a paying proposition.

The Millennium Dome might still have been undertaken even if the two governments had foreseen the outcome, though Gordon Brown reckoned it was one of the Blair government's 'mistakes'. The total cost budget was not very heavily overspent, though the net cost to government was twice the original plan. But in this case it seems that 'national prestige' carried a fairly heavy weighting. Probably an experienced operations manager should have been in charge from 1999 at latest.

So, in my view, given perfect foreknowledge, governments *might* still have chosen to proceed only with R.100 airships (not as a government-*run* project), with nuclear power on a smaller scale and with imported US technology for the second programme, and with the Dome.

Management

In their book *The Power Game*, Bruce-Gardyne and Lawson choose to focus on political aspects of 'decisions' as to whether to go ahead with four projects (Concorde being one of them). They do not discuss whether the decisions were 'right'. (Henderson deplored 'the unimportance of being right'[8] in affecting promotion in the civil service.) A related aspect (see Chapter 8) is whether or not (and when) to *abandon* projects. Possibly both Concorde and the Dome should have been cancelled, and perhaps the Attlee government should have called off the groundnut scheme *sooner* than it did. But large government projects lasting several years have a momentum of their own; and anyway they need more than go/no go decisions: they need *managing*.

Though politicians hog the limelight, behind the scenes senior civil servants have a strong influence. Indeed, in many ways they are 'more steadily and continuously important than their political bosses'.[9] But neither group consists of expert managers. There

8   P. D. Henderson, 'Two British errors: their probable size and some possible lessons', *Oxford Economic Papers*, 1977, p. 190.

9   C. P. Snow, *Science and Government*, Oxford University Press, 1961, p. 21.

seems to be a dilemma in government project management: either establish a complex, expensive and time-consuming precautionary system of checks and balances, or else take more risk by engaging a single leader to provide drive and focus.

In managing projects in progress, there are three essentials:

- Regular reviews, focusing on the latest estimates of the amount and timing of future cash inflows and outflows.
- Up-to-date market research to try to reassess likely demand where relevant.
- An 'exit champion' if need be, to argue the case for abandonment.

A sponsoring minister needs to 'hear' new information, however unwelcome. But people's 'body language' can reveal that they would rather *not* hear it. (That seems to have been one of Lord Thomson's mistakes with the R.101 airship.) Timeliness is often more important than accuracy, which is why *gossip* can be so useful to managers. No one wants bad news, but if the news *is* bad a project manager needs to be aware of it as soon as possible.

It seems hard to avoid the conclusion that none of the six projects was well managed. Many of these 'management' failures (though by no means all) were really down to politicians: publishing misleading estimates, installing inadequate or over-complex organisational arrangements, going ahead without a pilot scheme, appointing incompetent managers, overvaluing 'national prestige', insisting on excessive secrecy, funking abandonment, or generally interfering in details.

Many of the R.101 airship's technical aspects were never inde-pendently checked (what a contrast with Concorde!); costs seemed unimportant; the project overran on time by more than 100 per cent; owing to the overweight structure, passenger capacity was much less than specified; and in the end safety was blatantly ignored in order to meet a spurious political deadline. Thus the final flight trials lasted only 17 hours, not 48, there was no full-power trial and no bad-weather trial. Finally there was inexcusable ambiguity about who was actually in charge of the flight to India.

The groundnut scheme's management was poor, though the very concept of mechanisation was most unsuitable for East Africa. There was a failure to plan ahead with respect to infra-structure investment, or to investigate clearing and growing conditions; there were serious labour problems among both European and African workers, and maintenance of machines was hampered by the (predictable but not predicted) inexperience of drivers and mechanics. There were serious communication and authority problems between the Overseas Food Corporation (OFC) in London and local management in Kongwa. Even when, in the absence of a pilot scheme, the first season ended in almost complete disaster, there was a political reluctance to recognise the fact.

Nuclear power costs were never properly quantified; and governments accepted misleading Atomic Energy Authority (AEA) estimates throughout, with gross disregard of decommis-sioning costs. There was a panic trebling of the first programme after Suez. On both programmes the technical uncertainties and labour relations problems were little short of breathtaking, with long production delays and huge capital cost overruns. The Fast Breeder Reactor proved to be a very expensive failure. The consortia system did not work well, partly because the failure to replicate power stations meant doing without economies of scale.

Forecasting, both of consumer demand (too high) and of the supply of rival fuels (too low), was poor.

Concorde's cost estimates were much too low for a high-risk project on the frontiers of knowledge, with huge technical problems to overcome, especially concerning weight. There was little effort to estimate the size of the market and consider likely customer requirements until far too late. There was a failure to recognise environmental problems, both from noise on take-off and from sonic boom. The Anglo-French nature of the organisation was extremely cumbersome and expensive, with poorly structured incentives for contractors.

The Channel Tunnel's cost estimates were also much too low, owing to delays and design changes; and there were serious technical problems to deal with, partly with regard to the tunnelling but also on many aspects of systems and equipment. The safety arrangements may not have been cost-effective. There was a lack of trust between Eurotunnel, constructors and bankers. Customer demand forecasts were far too high, partly because of unforeseen competition from budget airlines and partly because a key part of the whole 'project' – the high-speed link between the Tunnel and London – was delayed for more than thirteen years. By no means were all of these things the government's fault.

The Millennium Dome was not a management triumph either, owing partly to top management's inexperience at running this sort of event. The 'checks and balances' were very messy and over-political. There was delay and confusion over the design and contents of the Dome; sponsorship was badly handled; the advance marketing was poor; the opening night was a fiasco; and the initial operations were marked by equipment breakdowns and very long queues (even though attendance was less than half that expected, not helped by the initial absence of ticket sales at the door). Financial forecasting and management were extremely poor throughout. The arrival of an experienced operations manager in February 2000 brought immediate and significant improvements.

Public choice theory

Given that, when governments are involved in resource allocation, decisions are guided by interest groups within government, Parliament, the civil service and the electorate, we would expect that there would be certain lessons deriving from 'public choice' theory.

The R.101 airship was the government entry 'competing' with private enterprise. The two aircraft were trying to meet the same specification; and while neither completely succeeded, the Vickers R.100 was at least able to fly to Canada and back, and cost about one third less than the government R.101, which crashed after a few hours of its demonstration flight to India. In this case, competition, rather than government 'enterprise', worked.

The government seems to have spent very little time thinking about the practicalities of the groundnut scheme, so urgent was the perceived need and so dazzling the prospect. Moreover, there were no triggers inside the government to cause anyone to look a bit harder before leaping. In this sense the decision to go ahead without any pilot scheme could be called irresponsible.

Nuclear power suffered badly from information asymmetry and from a small influential pressure group with much to gain from continued investment in the project. There also seems to have been a gung-ho attitude of 'we must have this British product *whatever* the cost' – indeed, nobody even knew the costs for very many years.

Concorde was clearly a production-oriented project; and constructing the supersonic transport was a splendid achievement. But the aircraft was extremely expensive both to build and to operate; and partly because of operating cost, partly because of aspects such as noise, no independent airlines were willing to buy it. Nobody seems to have cared very much about the potential *customers* for this product until far too late. The project was driven by the 'political marketplace' rather than the economic marketplace.

The Channel Tunnel (together with the CTRL) was another tremendous engineering feat; and although it cost about twice as much as planned, most of the excess was borne by investors in Eurotunnel, and much of the rest by the constructors of the Tunnel. Again, however, market estimates were very badly astray: in particular the reactions of two important competitors – the budget airlines and the ferries – were almost completely overlooked. The government part of the project, the Channel Tunnel high-speed rail link to London, was not ready for *thirteen years* after the Tunnel opened, and cost far more than expected. Part of this time overrun was caused by planning disputes regarding the route of the high-speed railway, together with decisions being taken by government to route the railway to facilitate regeneration. Again, these decisions were subject to the vagaries of the political rather than the commercial marketplace.

The Millennium Dome opened 'on time', though the contents were subject to serious problems, such as operating reliability and customer appeal. The main problem from the start was that the politicians wildly overestimated how many customers could be expected; and the inexperienced managers they appointed got many things wrong.

So in all three cases concerning customers who had a choice, those managing the government projects got it about as wrong as they possibly could have done. Politicians had invested none of their own *money*, and they hardly stood to lose *votes* if the projects failed, since electors would have so many other matters to take into account at the next general election. As a result the politicians didn't really *care* that much: they could 'afford' to be irresponsible. The costs of the projects were diffused over a large number of electors – no group of electors had an incentive to lobby against the projects as the cost of lobbying would have been much greater than the possible benefits from lobbying. In some cases, however, such as nuclear power, there were interest groups who had a strong interest in lobbying *in favour* of the continuation of the project. Ironically, in the one project where costs were concentrated on a particular group (homeowners in parts of Kent through which it was proposed that the high-speed railway would run), delays were caused by objections from that group and from their representatives in Parliament.

Conclusion

If everyone 'meant well', who was to blame: politicians, civil servants, scientists, engineers or managers? No, I think *what* was mainly to blame was the post-second-world-war collectivist *zeitgeist* – the visceral distrust of markets, partly based on ignorance, which I call 'agoraphobia'. This was especially true of the three projects starting within fifteen years of the end of World War II: the groundnut scheme, civil nuclear power and Concorde.

For the airship project, the notion of a 'competition' between government and private enterprise may have seemed attractive – even if the ultimate victor, private enterprise, was predictable. Mrs Thatcher and François Mitterrand robustly arranged for private enterprise to finance, build and operate the second Channel Tunnel: though such preference for a market solution did not fully carry over to the high-speed rail link to London. Both Conservative and Labour governments briefly considered abandoning the Millennium Dome: but in the end interventionist politicians – Heseltine and Prescott – could not resist throwing taxpayers' money at a 'prestige' project with environmental benefits.

In these projects, two basic business functions, producing and selling, both proved 'challenging'. Providing suitable incentives for contractors was difficult. Production was a disaster in the groundnut scheme; the overall *quality* of the Dome was dubious; and all the other four projects met with serious technical, cost and time problems. In three projects there was a need to sell the product. The number of customers was less than half the forecasts for the Channel Tunnel and the Millennium Dome – a huge shortfall. For Concorde (apart from two state-owned airlines), there were no 'outside' customers at all.

An important lesson from these projects is that governments do not *understand* product markets where customers are free to choose. Politicians and civil servants insist, Douglas-Jay-like,[10] on providing welfare services 'free' to the masses, but they take great care to see that most people have hardly any real choice.

---

10   Who famously said: 'In the case of nutrition and health, as in the case of education, the gentleman in Whitehall really does know better what is good for people than the people know themselves.' (Douglas Jay, *The Socialist Case*, Faber and Faber, London, 1948.)

Governments are not really 'monopolists', since they are not *selling* anything. One might call them 'monoparechists', single *providers*. They act like paternalists, not like competitors. This basic shortcoming, which seems unlikely to change, amounts to a fatal drawback for government projects involving direct sales to the public.

In the market system a useful rule of thumb is *'caveat emptor'* ('let the buyer take care'). A similar rule of thumb for governments might be: *'caveat gubernator'* ('let the government take care'). Before politicians decide to embark on a large quasi-commercial project they should provide convincing answers to two obvious questions:

- Why won't a private enterprise company undertake this project? (If it will, let it.)
- Why does *government*, in contrast, think the project worthwhile?

Large projects might benefit from having one or two official 'devil's advocates', who would have two main functions: to raise 'politically incorrect' questions, which (for example) contradict some of top management's assumptions; and to ask 'dumb' questions, admitting ignorance without any fear of 'looking stupid'. Here one needs independent-minded people of the sort Nevil Shute was talking about. It would be useful to have them around from the very start of a project. Then they could question its shape, basic assumptions and precise aims while they were still open to argument.

The role of devil's advocate aims to *legitimise* raising awkward points about a project. The task would be to point out all the risks

– what might go wrong, reductions in likely customer demand, etc. It also aims to counter complacency, such as appeared at times with the R.101 airship, the groundnut scheme, nuclear power stations and the Dome. Otherwise, especially with 'political' projects (which government projects will normally be), there may be intolerance of argument – a tendency to suggest that anyone who is not with us is against us.

Spencer[11] tells of a druggist's assistant who misinterprets a description of pains, prescribes the wrong medicine, kills the patient and is convicted of manslaughter. 'He is not allowed to excuse himself on the ground that he did not intend to kill the patient but hoped for good. ... He is told that he had no right to risk disastrous consequences by meddling in a matter concerning which his knowledge was so inadequate. The fact that he was ignorant of how great was his ignorance[12] is not accepted [as mitigation].' This story has an important message for governments.

My own 'solution' is simply: let the market work. To proceed with more large government quasi-commercial projects would be a recipe for further expensive disasters. Governments that lose thousands of millions of pounds of taxpayers' money should not easily be excused on the grounds that 'they meant well'. Those of us who advocate laissez-faire (which I define simply as 'government non-interference') mean well too.

---

11   Herbert Spencer, *The Man versus the State: The Sins of Legislators*, Penguin, Harmonds-worth, 1969, p. 115.

12   Donald Rumsfeld's 'unknown unknowns'.

Acronyms

AEA   Atomic Energy Authority
CTRL   Channel Tunnel Rail Link
NMEC   New Millennium Experience Company
OFC   Overseas Food Corporation
UAC   United Africa Company

APPENDIX 1
A NOTE ON SOURCES

R.101 airship

The 1931 Report of the Official Inquiry provides many of the basic facts. The two other main sources were Nevil Shute's 1954 autobiography *Slide Rule* and Sir Peter Masefield's book *To Ride the Storm*, published in 1982. Nevil Shute (Norway), the novelist, who was the R.100's chief engineer, was highly critical of the Cardington staff; while Sir Peter Masefield, formerly technical editor of *The Aeroplane* and chief executive of British European Airways, was extremely defensive of Lord Thomson. Neither is completely credible: the former because he downplays details of R.100's serious problems, the latter because he invents 'conversations' he cannot have heard (though he also includes a mass of useful statistics).

The groundnut scheme

Official sources include White Papers, especially the Wakefield Report itself, Hansard debates and the accounts of the Overseas Food Corporation (OFC). Alan Wood's 1950 book *The Ground Nut Affair* contained fascinating details, but few statistics, and appeared before the scheme finished. He had been the OFC's information officer and remained well disposed towards the idea, although he was critical of several practical aspects of the scheme. Also useful were S. Herbert Frankel's 1953 chapter 'The Kongwa experiment'; and more recently Jan S. Hogendorn and K. M. Scott's 1983 article 'The lessons of the East African groundnut scheme'; and Rizzo Matteo's 2005 doctoral thesis *The Groundnut Scheme Revisited*.

Nuclear power stations

Colin Robinson contributed substantially to this chapter, based on Chapters 1 and 3 of his 1991 book *The Power of the State*. Other useful sources were Margaret Gowing's 1974 two-volume *Independence and Deterrence: Britain and Atomic Energy 1945–1952*; Walter C. Patterson's 1976 book *Nuclear Power*; Duncan Burn's 1977 IEA Research Monograph *The Political Economy of Nuclear Energy*; David Henderson's 1977 article 'Two British errors: their probable size and some possible lessons'; and especially Roger Williams's 1980 book *The Nuclear Power Decisions: British Policies 1953–78*.

Concorde

There have been many books about Concorde. One of the most detailed is Kenneth Owen: *Concorde: Story of a supersonic pioneer*, a 2001 revision of his 1982 book. I have also drawn on David Henderson's 1977 article looking in detail at the costs and benefits of 'Two British errors'; Annabel May's 1979 article about foreign policy aspects; Peter Hall's 1980 book *Great Planning Disasters*, which has a chapter on Concorde; and Elliot J. Feldman's 1985 book *Concorde and Dissent: Explaining high technology project failures in Britain and France*.

The Channel Tunnel

The most detailed discussion is T. R. Gourvish's 2006 book *The Official History of Britain and the Channel Tunnel*, by the author of a recent history of British Rail. Some of the construction details come from Graham Anderson and Ben Rostrow's 1994 book *The Channel Tunnel Story* and Drew Fetherston's 1997 book *The Chunnel*. I have also consulted Eurotunnel's annual reports and accounts and two National Audit Office (NAO) reports on the Channel Tunnel Rail Link.

The Millennium Dome

Most of the basic financial and organisational facts are in the NAO report *The Millennium Dome* (9 November 2000). Further details appear in the NAO's *Winding-up the New Millennium Experience Company Limited* (17 April 2002); and the NAO's *English Partnerships: Regeneration of the Millennium Dome and Associated Land* (12 January 2005). Also helpful were Alastair Irvine's 1999 book *The Battle for the Millennium Dome* and Adam Nicolson's 1999 book *Regeneration: The Story of the Dome*. Both were published in the year before the Dome opened.

General

The most useful 'general' books have been John Jewkes's 1972 Wincott Lecture *Government and High Technology*; Peter Hall's *Great Planning Disasters* (1980); and Flyvjberg et al., *Megaprojects and Risk* (2003). After completing this book I came across *Business Blunders* by Geoff Tibbals (Robinson Publishing, 1999), which among many other short 'case studies' includes descriptions of both the R.101 airship and the groundnut scheme.

APPENDIX 2
A COMPLETE LIST OF ACRONYMS

AEA   Atomic Energy Authority
AGR   Advanced Gas-cooled Reactor
BA   British Airways
BAC   British Aircraft Corporation
BR   British Rail
BWR   Boiling Water Reactor (a type of LWR)
CEGB   Central Electricity Generating Board
CMS   (Department for) Culture, Media and Sport
CofA   Certificate of Airworthiness
CTG–FM   Channel Tunnel Group – France Manche
CTRL   Channel Tunnel Rail Link
DOE   Department of the Environment
DTI   Department of Trade and Industry
EIB   European Investment Bank
FBR   Fast Breeder Reactor
GEC   The General Electric Company Limited
GW   Gigawatts (a thousand million watts)
HWR   Heavy Water Reactor
IGC   Inter-Governmental Commission
JLE   Jubilee Line extension
LCR   London & Continental Railways
LWR   Light Water Reactor (either BWR or PWR)

MUC	Minimum Usage Charge
MW	Megawatts (a million watts)
NAO	National Audit Office
NFFO	Non Fossil Fuel Obligation
NII	Nuclear Installation Inspectorate
NMEC	New Millennium Experience Company
OFC	Overseas Food Corporation
ONS	Office of National Statistics
PFI	Private Finance Initiative
PWR	Pressurised Water Reactor (a type of LWR)
RAE	Royal Aircraft Establishment
SG-HWR	Steam Generating Heavy Water Reactor
SNCF	Société Nationale des Chemins de Fer Français
SSEB	South of Scotland Electricity Board
SST	Supersonic transport
STAC	Supersonic Transport Aircraft Committee
TAC	Tanganyika Agricultural Corporation
TBM	Tunnel-Boring Machine
THORP	Thermal Oxide Fuel Reprocessing Plant
TML	TransManche-Link
UAC	United Africa Company

ABOUT THE IEA

The Institute is a research and educational charity (No. CC 235 351), limited by guarantee. Its mission is to improve understanding of the fundamental institutions of a free society by analysing and expounding the role of markets in solving economic and social problems.

The IEA achieves its mission by:

- a high-quality publishing programme
- conferences, seminars, lectures and other events
- outreach to school and college students
- brokering media introductions and appearances

The IEA, which was established in 1955 by the late Sir Antony Fisher, is an educational charity, not a political organisation. It is independent of any political party or group and does not carry on activities intended to affect support for any political party or candidate in any election or referendum, or at any other time. It is financed by sales of publications, conference fees and voluntary donations.

In addition to its main series of publications the IEA also publishes a quarterly journal, *Economic Affairs*.

The IEA is aided in its work by a distinguished international Academic Advisory Council and an eminent panel of Honorary Fellows. Together with other academics, they review prospective IEA publications, their comments being passed on anonymously to authors. All IEA papers are therefore subject to the same rigorous independent refereeing process as used by leading academic journals.

IEA publications enjoy widespread classroom use and course adoptions in schools and universities. They are also sold throughout the world and often translated/reprinted.

Since 1974 the IEA has helped to create a worldwide network of 100 similar institutions in over 70 countries. They are all independent but share the IEA's mission.

Views expressed in the IEA's publications are those of the authors, not those of the Institute (which has no corporate view), its Managing Trustees, Academic Advisory Council members or senior staff.

Members of the Institute's Academic Advisory Council, Honorary Fellows, Trustees and Staff are listed on the following page.

The Institute gratefully acknowledges financial support for its publications programme and other work from a generous benefaction by the late Alec and Beryl Warren.

245

Other papers recently published by the IEA include:

WHO, What and Why?
Transnational Government, Legitimacy and the World Health Organization
Roger Scruton
Occasional Paper 113; ISBN 0 255 36487 3; £8.00

The World Turned Rightside Up
A New Trading Agenda for the Age of Globalisation
John C. Hulsman
Occasional Paper 114; ISBN 0 255 36495 4; £8.00

The Representation of Business in English Literature
Introduced and edited by Arthur Pollard
Readings 53; ISBN 0 255 36491 1; £12.00

Anti-Liberalism 2000
The Rise of New Millennium Collectivism
David Henderson
Occasional Paper 115; ISBN 0 255 36497 0; £7.50

Capitalism, Morality and Markets
Brian Griffiths, Robert A. Sirico, Norman Barry & Frank Field
Readings 54; ISBN 0 255 36496 2; £7.50

A Conversation with Harris and Seldon
Ralph Harris & Arthur Seldon
Occasional Paper 116; ISBN 0 255 36498 9; £7.50

Malaria and the DDT Story
Richard Tren & Roger Bate
Occasional Paper 117; ISBN 0 255 36499 7; £10.00

A Plea to Economists Who Favour Liberty: Assist the Everyman
Daniel B. Klein
Occasional Paper 118; ISBN 0 255 36501 2; £10.00

The Changing Fortunes of Economic Liberalism
Yesterday, Today and Tomorrow
David Henderson
Occasional Paper 105 (new edition); ISBN 0 255 36520 9; £12.50

The Global Education Industry
Lessons from Private Education in Developing Countries
James Tooley
Hobart Paper 141 (new edition); ISBN 0 255 36503 9; £12.50

Saving Our Streams
*The Role of the Anglers' Conservation Association in
Protecting English and Welsh Rivers*
Roger Bate
Research Monograph 53; ISBN 0 255 36494 6; £10.00

Better Off Out?
The Benefits or Costs of EU Membership
Brian Hindley & Martin Howe
Occasional Paper 99 (new edition); ISBN 0 255 36502 0; £10.00

Buckingham at 25
Freeing the Universities from State Control
Edited by James Tooley
Readings 55; ISBN 0 255 36512 8; £15.00

Lectures on Regulatory and Competition Policy
Irwin M. Stelzer
Occasional Paper 120; ISBN 0 255 36511 X; £12.50

Misguided Virtue
False Notions of Corporate Social Responsibility
David Henderson
Hobart Paper 142; ISBN 0 255 36510 1; £12.50

HIV and Aids in Schools
The Political Economy of Pressure Groups and Miseducation
Barrie Craven, Pauline Dixon, Gordon Stewart & James Tooley
Occasional Paper 121; ISBN 0 255 36522 5; £10.00

The Road to Serfdom
The Reader's Digest *condensed version*
Friedrich A. Hayek
Occasional Paper 122; ISBN 0 255 36530 6; £7.50

Bastiat's *The Law*
Introduction by Norman Barry
Occasional Paper 123; ISBN 0 255 36509 8; £7.50

A Globalist Manifesto for Public Policy
Charles Calomiris
Occasional Paper 124; ISBN 0 255 36525 X; £7.50

Euthanasia for Death Duties
Putting Inheritance Tax Out of Its Misery
Barry Bracewell-Milnes
Research Monograph 54; ISBN 0 255 36513 6; £10.00

Liberating the Land
The Case for Private Land-use Planning
Mark Pennington
Hobart Paper 143; ISBN 0 255 36508 x; £10.00

IEA Yearbook of Government Performance 2002/2003
Edited by Peter Warburton
Yearbook 1; ISBN 0 255 36532 2; £15.00

Britain's Relative Economic Performance, 1870–1999
Nicholas Crafts
Research Monograph 55; ISBN 0 255 36524 1; £10.00

Should We Have Faith in Central Banks?
Otmar Issing
Occasional Paper 125; ISBN 0 255 36528 4; £7.50

The Dilemma of Democracy
Arthur Seldon
Hobart Paper 136 (reissue); ISBN 0 255 36536 5; £10.00

Capital Controls: a 'Cure' Worse Than the Problem?
Forrest Capie
Research Monograph 56; ISBN 0 255 36506 3; £10.00

The Poverty of 'Development Economics'
Deepak Lal
Hobart Paper 144 (reissue); ISBN 0 255 36519 5; £15.00

Should Britain Join the Euro?
The Chancellor's Five Tests Examined
Patrick Minford
Occasional Paper 126; ISBN 0 255 36527 6; £7.50

Post-Communist Transition: Some Lessons
Leszek Balcerowicz
Occasional Paper 127; ISBN 0 255 36533 0; £7.50

A Tribute to Peter Bauer
John Blundell et al.
Occasional Paper 128; ISBN 0 255 36531 4; £10.00

Employment Tribunals
Their Growth and the Case for Radical Reform
J. R. Shackleton
Hobart Paper 145; ISBN 0 255 36515 2; £10.00

Fifty Economic Fallacies Exposed
Geoffrey E. Wood
Occasional Paper 129; ISBN 0 255 36518 7; £12.50

A Market in Airport Slots
Keith Boyfield (editor), David Starkie, Tom Bass & Barry Humphreys
Readings 56; ISBN 0 255 36505 5; £10.00

Money, Inflation and the Constitutional Position of the Central Bank
Milton Friedman & Charles A. E. Goodhart
Readings 57; ISBN 0 255 36538 1; £10.00

railway.com
Parallels between the Early British Railways and the ICT Revolution
Robert C. B. Miller
Research Monograph 57; ISBN 0 255 36534 9; £12.50

The Regulation of Financial Markets
Edited by Philip Booth & David Currie
Readings 58; ISBN 0 255 36551 9; £12.50

Climate Alarmism Reconsidered
Robert L. Bradley Jr
Hobart Paper 146; ISBN 0 255 36541 1; £12.50

Government Failure: E. G. West on Education
Edited by James Tooley & James Stanfield
Occasional Paper 130; ISBN 0 255 36552 7; £12.50

Corporate Governance: Accountability in the Marketplace
Elaine Sternberg
Second edition
Hobart Paper 147; ISBN 0 255 36542 x; £12.50

The Land Use Planning System
Evaluating Options for Reform
John Corkindale
Hobart Paper 148; ISBN 0 255 36550 0; £10.00

Economy and Virtue
Essays on the Theme of Markets and Morality
Edited by Dennis O'Keeffe
Readings 59; ISBN 0 255 36504 7; £12.50

Free Markets Under Siege
Cartels, Politics and Social Welfare
Richard A. Epstein
Occasional Paper 132; ISBN 0 255 36553 5; £10.00

Unshackling Accountants
D. R. Myddelton
Hobart Paper 149; ISBN 0 255 36559 4; £12.50

The Euro as Politics
Pedro Schwartz
Research Monograph 58; ISBN 0 255 36535 7; £12.50

Pricing Our Roads
Vision and Reality
Stephen Glaister & Daniel J. Graham
Research Monograph 59; ISBN 0 255 36562 4; £10.00

The Role of Business in the Modern World
Progress, Pressures, and Prospects for the Market Economy
David Henderson
Hobart Paper 150; ISBN 0 255 36548 9; £12.50

Public Service Broadcasting Without the BBC?
Alan Peacock
Occasional Paper 133; ISBN 0 255 36565 9; £10.00

The ECB and the Euro: the First Five Years
Otmar Issing
Occasional Paper 134; ISBN 0 255 36555 1; £10.00

Towards a Liberal Utopia?
Edited by Philip Booth
Hobart Paperback 32; ISBN 0 255 36563 2; £15.00

The Way Out of the Pensions Quagmire
Philip Booth & Deborah Cooper
Research Monograph 60; ISBN 0 255 36517 9; £12.50

Black Wednesday
A Re-examination of Britain's Experience in the Exchange Rate Mechanism
Alan Budd
Occasional Paper 135; ISBN 0 255 36566 7; £7.50

Crime: Economic Incentives and Social Networks
Paul Ormerod
Hobart Paper 151; ISBN 0 255 36554 3; £10.00

The Road to Serfdom *with* **The Intellectuals and Socialism**
Friedrich A. Hayek
Occasional Paper 136; ISBN 0 255 36576 4; £10.00

Money and Asset Prices in Boom and Bust
Tim Congdon
Hobart Paper 152; ISBN 0 255 36570 5; £10.00

The Dangers of Bus Re-regulation
and Other Perspectives on Markets in Transport
John Hibbs et al.
Occasional Paper 137; ISBN 0 255 36572 1; £10.00

The New Rural Economy
Change, Dynamism and Government Policy
Berkeley Hill et al.
Occasional Paper 138; ISBN 0 255 36546 2; £15.00

The Benefits of Tax Competition
Richard Teather
Hobart Paper 153; ISBN 0 255 36569 1; £12.50

Wheels of Fortune
Self-funding Infrastructure and the Free Market Case for a Land Tax
Fred Harrison
Hobart Paper 154; ISBN 0 255 36589 6; £12.50

Were 364 Economists All Wrong?
Edited by Philip Booth
Readings 60; ISBN 978 0 255 36588 8; £10.00

Europe After the 'No' Votes
Mapping a New Economic Path
Patrick A. Messerlin
Occasional Paper 139; ISBN 978 0 255 36580 2; £10.00

The Railways, the Market and the Government
John Hibbs et al.
Readings 61; ISBN 978 0 255 36567 3; £12.50

Corruption: The World's Big C
Cases, Causes, Consequences, Cures
Ian Senior
Research Monograph 61; ISBN 978 0 255 36571 0; £12.50

Choice and the End of Social Housing
Peter King
Hobart Paper 155; ISBN 978 0 255 36568 0; £10.00

Sir Humphrey's Legacy
Facing Up to the Cost of Public Sector Pensions
Neil Record
Hobart Paper 156; ISBN 978 0 255 36578 9; £10.00

The Economics of Law
Cento Veljanovski
Second edition
Hobart Paper 157; ISBN 978 0 255 36561 1; £12.50

Living with Leviathan
Public Spending, Taxes and Economic Performance
David B. Smith
Hobart Paper 158; ISBN 978 0 255 36579 6; £12.50

The Vote Motive
Gordon Tullock
New edition
Hobart Paperback 33; ISBN 978 0 255 36577 2; £10.00

Waging the War of Ideas
John Blundell
Third edition
Occasional Paper 131; ISBN 978 0 255 36606 9; £12.50

The War Between the State and the Family
How Government Divides and Impoverishes
Patricia Morgan
Hobart Paper 159; ISBN 978 0 255 36596 3; £10.00

Capitalism – A Condensed Version
Arthur Seldon
Occasional Paper 140; ISBN 978 0 255 36598 7; £7.50

Catholic Social Teaching and the Market Economy
Edited by Philip Booth
Hobart Paperback 34; ISBN 978 0 255 36581 9; £15.00

Adam Smith – A Primer
Eamonn Butler
Occasional Paper 141; ISBN 978 0 255 36608 3; £7.50

Happiness, Economics and Public Policy
Helen Johns & Paul Ormerod
Research Monograph 62; ISBN 978 0 255 36600 7; £10.00

All the listed IEA papers, including those that are out of print, can be downloaded from www.iea.org.uk. Purchases can also be made through the website. To order copies of currently available IEA papers, or to enquire about availability, please contact:

Gazelle
IEA orders
FREEPOST RLYS-EAHU-YSCZ
White Cross Mills
Hightown
Lancaster LA1 4XS

Tel: 01524 68765
Fax: 01524 63232
Email: sales@gazellebooks.co.uk

The IEA also offers a subscription service to its publications. For a single annual payment, currently £42.00 in the UK, you will receive every monograph the IEA publishes during the course of a year and discounts on our extensive back catalogue. For more information, please contact:

Adam Myers
Subscriptions
The Institute of Economic Affairs
2 Lord North Street
London SW1P 3LB

Tel: 020 7799 8920
Fax: 020 7799 2137
Website: www.iea.org.uk

They Meant Well

Government Project Disasters